Leadership - The Heart Matters

Laurie Hinzman

Copyright © 2010 by Laurie Hinzman. All rights reserved. Printed in the United States of America. Except as permitted under the Copyright Act of 1976, no part of this publication may be reproduced or distributed in any form or by any means, or stored in a database or retrieval system, without the prior written permission of the author. www.leadershiptheheartmatters.com.

ISBN 13/EAN 13.   9781452869742
Editor: Evelyn Alemanni (www.allea.com)
Book design and layout: Evelyn Alemanni
Cover illustration: Wayne Wilcoxen

About the Author

Laurie Hinzman, MA is a well-respected school principal and leadership coach in San Diego, CA. She began her career in 1980 and has extensive and diverse experience in education, consulting, coaching, management, and leadership. Mrs. Hinzman has honed her leadership approach–leading from the heart – throughout her career and it applies to anyone, anywhere, who undertakes a leadership role in life. Her approach has been lauded by colleagues and widely adopted by leaders and educators whom she mentors.

Mrs. Hinzman was recently honored with the regional "2010 Administrator of the Year" award.

She lives in Poway, California with her husband, Bob.

Acknowledgements

Many people have influenced my understanding of leading from the heart—my heartfelt thanks and gratitude to them. Leading is only possible when there are team members to work with, to provide feedback, and to share life lessons. My appreciation to those I have had the pleasure to work with.

My deepest gratitude goes to my husband, Bob, who has been my biggest fan, unconditionally. His belief, encouragement, and support in my ability to achieve my vision to write this book never wavered. You are my rock—from my heart—my love forever!

Thank you to Dr. Barbara MacNeil, whose knowledge and passion for education provided many professional opportunities for me. She believed in and nurtured my leadership ability from the first time I met her in 1983. She was my mentor and friend.

Dedication

This book is dedicated to my Dad and Mom whose core beliefs about approaching life with integrity, fairness, zest, and heart provided the foundation from which I live my life. Their selfless acts opened many doors for lifelong experiences and opportunities. The strength and encouragement they shared gave me confidence in achieving my goals. They are missed but live forever, with love, in my heart.

Contents

About the Author 2
Acknowledgements 3
Dedication 5
Preface 11
Introduction 13
   Why the heart? 13
   Leadership - what is it? 14
   Leading vs. managing 15
   What is leading with the heart? 17
   Intuition vs. experience 17
      Compassion vs. coldness 18
      Passion vs. emotion 18
      Wisdom vs. knowledge 19
      Cooperation and collaboration 19
   What happens when you lead with heart
   (outcomes and benefits) 20
   Leadership with heart can be heart-healthy 20
   How to practice leadership with heart 20
   Components of leadership with heart 21

Empowerment 23
   Create shared visions and goals 24
   Go public with visions, goals, dreams, and beliefs 28
   Encourage risk-taking with reflection and
   accountability 30
   Create an environment where people want to
   participate with full hearts 34

Keep an open heart, open mind…open door 39
Celebrate the work dance 41
Celebrate and appreciate 44

Character 49
Attitude 50
Honesty 53
Courage 57
Perseverance 60
Respect 62
Giving 66

Integrity 69
Stay true to the heart of the work 70
Never compromise your integrity 73
Make an absolute and unconditional commitment 76
Advocate equity and fairness 79
Promote with integrity 81
Practice transparency 83
Recognize when it's time to move on 85

Voice 89
Dialogue with heart 90
Talking with instead of talking at 93
Choose words carefully, strategically 95
Carry the message with clarity, firmness,
and respect 98
Understand defensiveness 100

Laughter is the best medicine 103

Delivery 105

Body talk 110

Tone 112

Writing etiquette 114

Model **119**

Practice what you preach...walk the talk 120

Own your behavior 123

Learn from mistakes 126

Solution vs. problem 129

Project a professional image 132

First impressions, manners, and etiquette 136

Guide **141**

Heart-to-heart 143

Guide according to the big picture 145

Coach with greatness and success in mind 147

Keep expectations high and realistic 150

Sage on the stage vs. guide on the side 152

Emotion vs. passion and professionalism 154

Listen with a full heart, watch, and take notes 157

Feedback–firm, inquisitive, thought-provoking 162

Redirect with suggestions, accountability,
and timelines 163

Reflection 167

Reflection vs. reaction 170

Confidence... 173
    Experience... 174
    Confidence without arrogance............................... 178
    Nurture confidence in others.................................. 182
    Believe... 185
    Lifelong learning.. 187
    Teachable moments 190

Preface

Leaders and followers—they're simply a fact of the human condition. You've experienced born leaders—the child who gets everyone to play a certain game or the boss who you would do anything for. You've also, no doubt, experienced people who think they're leaders, but in fact, are just dictators. Maybe you've had opportunities to lead and wondered how to go about it.

Every group or organization has leaders...good, bad, or indifferent. Leadership style affects not just those who are "led", but the leaders as well. Hundreds of tomes have been written on leadership and leadership style. This book takes a new approach—leading with, and from, the heart. It is an approach I developed based on my years in the education field and incorporates proven methods for building heart-healthy teams of people who embrace their work with passion, enthusiasm, creativity, and excitement. Remarkably, just as I was finishing the first draft of this book, I was honored with the "Administrator of the Year" award from the Association of California School Administrators Region 18 (San Diego and Imperial Counties). That was certainly a validation that leading from the heart does work and is appreciated!

This book is intended for anyone in a leadership position, whether it's a volunteer organization, scout troop, governmental entity, or a multi-national business. Wherever, whoever, or whatever you're leading, the guiding principles are the same.

Leading from the heart means building on learning, experience, and knowledge with compassion, intuition, and reflection. Leading from the heart takes work. It means empowering and trusting a team and giving them the freedom to do the job creatively, to explore new solutions and to make mistakes and learn from them. Consider this book a resource for developing your own leadership style, and for growing as an individual as well as a leader.

Perhaps it is because of my years in education that I added "Gentle Reminders" throughout the chapters. Their purpose is to allow you to stop, reflect, and think about the concept and how it relates to your leadership practice. I also created "Reflections", a workbook component. Why? Because just as reading books about diet and exercise without actually changing your lifestyle won't change your body, reading a book on leadership without reflecting and putting the concepts into practice won't make you a better leader.

Take time with this book—it's not meant to be a fast read. Use the workbook segments to reflect on each topic and enhance your own leadership practice and experiences. You may find that you want to write out the answers to each reflection question and review them periodically to see how you have grown in your leadership practice.

So, lead well, lead brilliantly, lead with greatness, and lead from the heart!

~Laurie Hinzman

introduction

> Leadership is not so much about technique and methods as it is about opening the heart. Leadership is about inspiration—of oneself and of others. Great leadership is about human experiences, not processes. Leadership is not a formula or a program, it is a human activity that comes from the heart and considers the hearts of others. It is an attitude, not a routine.
> *~Lance Secretan*

There are those who lead, then there are those who lead from the heart. This book is about leading from the heart and describes in detail my seven principles of heart-healthy leadership.

Why the heart?

At the inner core of all people is "heart"—not the physical organ, but the center of one's personality, the center of character and emotional life. "Heart" drives feelings, emotions, intuitions, actions, and reactions. Using the heart is part of the process of truly understanding the whole of a problem or situation. Emotions, led by the heart, dictate how we interact with others…no matter age, experience, profession, problem, etc. Emotions play a huge part in perception, results and outcomes. The heart lies deep within our souls and is the essence of our spirit, courage, and enthusiasm.

Heart Healthy Leadership

The conventional geometrical depiction of a heart symbolizes unity, wholeness, and connectedness. It is almost the exact opposite of the typical top-down hierarchical organizational structure. Leading with heart is what gives us the ability to encourage greatness, cheer people on, build confidence in others, believe unconditionally, model, give trust, and create a non-threatening work and learning environment.

Scientifically speaking, without a heart (the organ) we would not be…it is the essential body part, the strongest muscle, it gives us life every day. In its body function, the heart is the core that pumps the blood that keeps our bodies healthy and strong. The power of the heart is life…we need to nurture it so it continues to give us life.

We are told over and over again to take care of our biological heart through exercise and nutrition to give it longevity and strength. By using the "heart" as a guide when facilitating, making decisions, working towards goals and visions, collaborating, etc., we are in fact putting into practice the same idea: exercise (using the heart as your guide) and nutrition (using the heart to "feed", encourage, energize) those around you so they in turn will give their hearts to their work.

Leadership - what is it?

Leadership is much more an art, a belief, a condition of the heart, than a set of things to do. The visible signs of artful leadership are expressed, ultimately, in its practice. ~Max DePree

Leadership is the ability to encourage, engage, excite, empower, and energize people to the point where their collective decisions and practices lead to positive and desired outcomes. Effective leadership, or the lack of it, influences the overall health and success of an organization. Effective leadership creates a work environment where people want to do their personal best, not because you want them to but because they want to. It is not about power, it's about empowerment which includes your heart and the heart of others, unconditionally. Effective leadership inspires, enlists and trusts the inspiration, innovation, and creativity of others.

Leadership is not dictatorship. A dictatorial, top down, hierarchical style of management is a reflection of individuals working alone who typically feel they are above all others. Leadership is not a self-promoting act, it is an act that brings out the best in people by promoting the abilities, knowledge, and skills of others without threat. Leadership is collaboration and teamwork that work towards achieving common visions and goals.

Effective leadership is a skill that positively influences and impacts relationships. Its foundation is built from a strong core belief and value system fueled by passion, dedication, integrity, and rightness. Effective leadership is not the result of political and personal agendas because it is grounded in wisdom, intuition, compassion, and confidence.

Leadership does not require a person to have multiple academic degrees. Although degrees are honorable, a piece of paper doesn't make a person an effective leader. It's about what's inside of you, your core beliefs, values, wisdom, and knowledge about people, life, and the future.

Leadership opportunities are available to all of us throughout our lives and are part of character development that begins at a very early age. Leadership practice evolves and takes shape if we pay attention to lessons learned throughout lifelong experiences. It can be learned if you have an open heart and mind.

Leading vs. managing

Good leaders make people feel that they're at the very heart of things, not at the periphery. Everyone feels that he or she makes a difference to the success of the organization. When that happens, people feel centered and that gives their work meaning. ~Warren Bennis

Management is doing things right; leadership is doing the right things.
~Peter F. Drucker

Managing is to power of self as Leadership is to empower of self and others.
~Laurie Hinzman

Through many years of observing and experiencing "leaders" I have identified the following leadership styles which differentiate between a true leader, a manager, and a follower:

1. Innate (Leader)   Walks the talk; will not compromise integrity to support political and personal agendas; sees the big picture (future); collaborates; thinks outside the box; leads with heart—unconditionally; empowers; considers the hearts of others; self-empowers without arrogance; and challenges mediocrity/status quo. An innate leader uses the four "R's" essential in leadership: revisit, reflect, revise, and re-energize.

2. Textbook (Managerial)
Talks the talk; changes with the tide (flavor of the day, latest management book, etc.); trend-follower to look progressive; false sense of knowledge; speaks from the text or opinion of others, not from personal wisdom, knowledge, and experience; follows a list of things to do; controls.

3. Puppet (Follower)
Whatever you want me to do—I'll do; people pleaser regardless of the greater good; compromises own beliefs to get ahead; wants to be the hero; satisfied with status quo; lacks self-confidence; controlled and manipulated by superiors. May control and manipulate others.

The textbook "leadership" style is a director of the work whether they believe in the work or not...it reflects a managing style fueled by trends, someone else's words or directives from above. Many definitions of the word "manager" start with the word "one"...one who controls, one who is in charge....The mere mention and use of the word "one" paired with the words "control" or "in charge" implies a unilateral practice.

The difference between managing (textbook) and leadership (innate) is that managing is the "using" of position, power, and control to achieve results while leadership is the sharing and distribution of position (creating leaders among the work force), power (empower), and control (innovation) in achieving results. Textbook "leadership" is a managerial style that can hinder the progressive thinking and creativity among team members. To manage is to tell people what to do and when to get it done. Though we are bound by deeds and timelines, being the "teller" of how to get there will inhibit employee confidence and trust in you as a leader. Textbook managing enables micromanaging, which stifles initiative and suppresses motivation. People who feel the need to micromanage often feel they know the best way to arrive at solutions and results. They are the people who need to have their hands in all the pies—creating an environment that diminishes trust in the expertise of the team.

Innate leadership is to show the way, to guide people in a set direction, but not tell them every step. True leadership challenges status quo by trusting team members to get the job done, using their knowledge and skills without hand-holding. Leading is directing and facilitating...managing is controlling and commanding.

A "leader" who follows (puppet) stands behind others to get the job done. They may have the position of authority but their actions are driven by the decisions, opinions, and directives of the higher ups. Puppet "leaders" typically have low self-confidence and a limited knowledge base or experience to lead the work. They are often the ones who have been promoted to their level of incompetence (the Peter Principle).

What is leading with the heart?

The heart is the first feature of working minds. ~Frank Lloyd Wright

"Leading" is setting a direction towards the achievement of goals.... "Leading with heart" is setting a direction towards the achievement of goals by creating synergy among team members based on common values, beliefs, visions and goals. How you get there matters...people matter regardless of the capacity in which they serve in the organization...relationships matter. Leading with heart takes into consideration the hearts of others. It's easy for people to say they "lead" their people but just plain leading can be confused with managing.

Desired results will happen faster and more efficiently when there is collective buy-in. Collective buy-in comes from relationship building where people are empowered and motivated to perform their jobs with a full heart. Taking care of your people brings the act of "leading" into leadership—this is the heart work.

Intuition vs. experience

The heart has reasons that reason does not understand.
                                            ~Jacques Bénigne Bossuel

There is no instinct like that of the heart. ~Lord Byron

Introduction

It's always with excitement that I wake up in the morning wondering what my intuition will toss up to me, like gifts from the sea. I work with it and rely on it. It is my partner. ~Dr. Jonas Salk

Experience is learned, intuition is innate—something we are born with. Leading with heart is trusting who you are as a person, inside and out. It's the ability to believe that your core beliefs and values are solid and grounded. Our intuition is driven by inner energy...gut feelings that influence decisions. Our intuition helps us make connections between emotions and reality. Pay attention and trust your intuitions when faced with the opportunities and possibilities of each day. Using your experience as a guide in leadership is part of the picture, using your intuition to execute decisions brings the heart into leadership. No matter how much experience you have, if you do not trust and use your own instincts in your professional practice then the act of leadership becomes an act of management.

Compassion vs. coldness

Leading with heart takes into consideration the hearts and feelings of others, above your own, which entails compassion. A leader who leads with heart understands that people have life stories that influence and impact their daily lives. Taking time to listen, understand, and show you care are heart qualities. When people feel that you, as their leader, care, then they will respect you more and acknowledge that you have a heart. If they think you don't care then they won't care. Coldness is not a characteristic to be proud of in any situation. Treat people the way you wish to be treated and you will find a team (organization) grounded in mutual respect.

Passion vs. emotion

Never confuse emotion with passion. ~Laurie Hinzman

Leading with heart includes passion, which is your conscious energy and enthusiasm for the work. Passion is your own inner love, conviction, and commitment for the work that needs to be accomplished. When using passion as your guide, you will lead to inspire, motivate, energize, and elicit intellectual excitement. Using your own enthusiasm to facilitate greatness within your organization is contagious and part of heart leadership. Decisions driven by passion exemplify a deep interest, commitment, and dedication to the work.

Emotions are generally spontaneous and can cloud judgment, leading to irrational and negative behavior. Passion should never be misinterpreted or confused with emotion. They are two separate feelings that send different messages. Passion can be stronger than emotion because it is fueled by unwavering energy and commitment. Passion will be the key to results as it sets an example that you are giving your time and energy unconditionally because of something you truly believe in. Let your passion, not emotions, drive your actions.

Wisdom vs. knowledge

The heart is wiser than the intellect. ~J.G. Holland

The heart, which is part of wisdom, is wiser than intelligence. Intelligence is nurtured by knowledge which builds wisdom. Knowledge encompasses learning and thoughts from other people, wisdom is what we do with knowledge. Wisdom is shaped by your life experiences; it is knowing what to do and being able to differentiate between good and bad. Leadership with heart is tapping into your inner self to guide and facilitate by doing the right things (wisdom).

Cooperation and collaboration

The leaders who work most effectively, it seems to me, never say "I." And that's not because they have trained themselves not to say "I." They don't think "I." They think "we"; they think "team". They understand their job to be to make the team function. They accept responsibility and don't sidestep it, but "we" gets the credit.... This is what creates trust, what enables you to get the task done. ~Peter F. Drucker

You can buy a person's hands but you can't buy his heart. His heart is where his enthusiasm, his loyalty is. ~Stephen Covey

Leading with heart is about cooperation and collaboration, using the best talents of everyone on your team. This practice brings more professionalism to an effort and raises the level of what can be achieved. The leader with heart creates synergy and excitement by bringing out the best in everyone.

What happens when you lead with heart (outcomes and benefits)

Your vision will become clear only when you look into your heart....Who looks outside, dreams. Who looks inside, awakens. ~Carl Jung

It is the heart that makes a man rich. He is rich according to what he is, not according to what he has. ~Henry Ward Beecher

True creativity quite simply starts with balancing your emotions and activating the power of the heart. Through practicing emotional management from the heart, you tap into the highest form of creativity possible—recreating your perceptions of reality. Creating a joint venture between head and heart puts a power pack behind your goals. Getting your head in sync with your heart and harnessing the power of coherence gives you the energy efficiency you need to achieve changes that haven't been possible before. The head can notice what things need to change, but the heart provides the power and direction to actually bring about the changes.... ~Doc Childre

Leading with heart and leading from the heart has the potential to make you a more effective leader, to make your job easier, and to affect team members in the same way. It will create an energized, synergized workplace where decisions are made based on trust and shared visions, goals, and priorities.

Leadership with "heart" can be heart-healthy

Leading with the heart as a guide can create a heart-healthy workplace. When the team works collaboratively and constructively toward a common goal and vision, workplace or organizational stress is reduced, which is healthy for your biological heart as well as your "heart".

How to practice leadership with heart

The ability to lead is an innate quality that only gets better with experience because true leaders focus on a path of continuous improvement. True leaders reflect on their work every step of the way and refine their skill set accordingly to achieve the best results. Effective leaders build and possess confidence without a display of arrogance. They have an innate talent with a strong core value system and the dedication and drive to implement strategies with integrity as an all-important initial foundation. True leaders do not waiver from their values to support political and personal agendas.

Components of leadership with heart

It seems that good things come in sevens, for example, the seven seas, seven continents, seven days of the week, and Seven Wonders of the World. So, too, come the seven principles of leading from the heart: empowerment, character, integrity, voice, model, guide, and confidence. These seven pillars don't stand alone. You might visualize each of these as a ribbon and weave them together to create a beautiful tapestry. Each of these principles is described in detail in the following chapters.

Empowerment

> Leaders who empower others bring joy, enthusiasm, and optimism to those lives they touch every day. A heart-healthy leader expects and empowers people to believe in themselves and builds relationships based on dignity, integrity, and respect.
> ~Laurie Hinzman

empowerment

> Believing leads to empowerment. Empowerment fuels confidence. Confidence: the foundation for personal best, success, and results.
> ~Laurie Hinzman

Empowerment is the leadership practice that enables people to perform to their potential, which leads to success and prosperity within an organization. To a leader, empowering someone means to endow that person with the authority and responsibility to make decisions; hold them accountable for the outcome, and to acknowledge and praise their efforts. This can enable greatness. Our job as leaders with heart is to empower people to perform to their potential, believe they can and will succeed. Leaders who empower engage in the following essential activities:

- Create shared visions and goals
- Go public with visions, goals, dreams, and beliefs
- Encourage risk-taking with reflection and accountability
- Create an environment where people want to participate with full hearts
- Keep an open heart, open mind...open door
- Celebrate the work dance
- Celebrate and appreciate

Create shared visions and goals

When a collection of brilliant minds, hearts, and talents come together . . . expect a masterpiece. ~Brilliance

Leadership is about capturing the imagination and enthusiasm of your people with clearly defined goals that cut through the fog like a beacon in the night.
~Leadership, Successories LLC

The vision must be followed by the venture. It is not enough to stare up the steps—we must step up the stairs. ~Vance Havne

Empowerment begs the question—empowered to do what? Empowerment requires that a group has shared visions and goals and that they are clearly articulated and understood.

The hierarchical, top down, unilateral leadership style creates fragmentation when it comes to implementing and achieving visions and goals. Unlike a hierarchical approach, empowering leaders work <u>with</u> their groups to identify core beliefs and create shared visions and goals to ensure a collaborative process and buy-in. An empowering leader makes this a daily practice to ensure total buy-in from the hearts of team members in achieving desired outcomes.

There must be a unified quest to setting standards based on common core values and beliefs—it cannot be a divided front. Focused efforts on creating shared visions, goals, and high expectations (with an understanding that all members are responsible for meeting them) will create a culture of success. The vision needs to be collaboratively agreed upon.

An empowered leader will facilitate and coach groups by including all members in the process of identifying common core beliefs and establishing the vision and goals for the work. An empowered leader will work to assure that the group's visions and goals align with those of the organization. The visions and goals must be inclusive and integrated across all levels and departments of the organization. When people have a "say-so" there is "buy-in", which leads to successful outcomes and supports a healthy future.

An empowering leader trusts team members and facilitates collaborative decision-making and problem solving to accelerate productivity.

Clear and concise guidelines that align with the visions need to be established collaboratively with the team to promote the understanding that all members are accountable for outcomes and results. There needs to be alignment among departments to develop progressive plans to move the work forward. A leader's active participation in problem-solving can help build a collaborative and unified work environment.

Gentle Reminder:

Visions and goals will get bigger when leaders instill the belief that the possibility of accomplishing a specific goal exists.

Reflections:

- What are your visions and goals for yourself and for the organization?

- How do your visions and goals contribute to the success of the entire organization?

- What's the difference between a dream and a goal?

- Do you know the core beliefs of the people you lead?

- Do you have collaborative visions and goals in place or are they something you created yourself or inherited and "assumed" to be mutually agreed upon?

- Have you differentiated between short and long-term goals?

- In a hierarchical organization, what is the potential for creativity?

- What kinds of decisions did you make today? Were they based on input/conversations from team members or were they unilateral? "My way or the highway?"

Go public with visions, goals, dreams, and beliefs

Once a group has decided on its visions and goals, these should be shared with the community (clients) served. Create a professional way (not just paper hanging on the wall) of displaying your visions and goals around your workplace, inside and out, so everyone can develop a collective understanding of what your organization represents. Post them on your website, in offices, conference rooms, lunchrooms, etc. Talk about them in meetings and informal discussions. Add them to written documents and integrate them into your phone conversations and sales pitches. Making everyone aware of the direction you are taking and expectations for all members of the organization will develop an appreciation for and understanding of your work. Going public with the expected outcomes and results will empower others to buy in to the work as well. Talk the talk with enthusiasm, passion, belief, and heart.

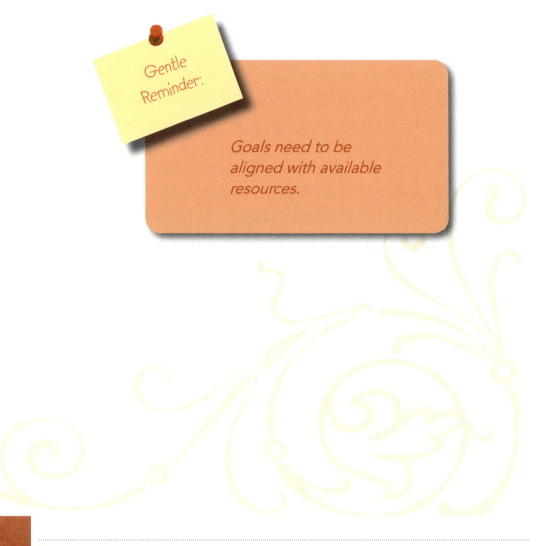

Gentle Reminder:

Goals need to be aligned with available resources.

Empowerment

Reflections:

- How does your group communicate its visions, goals, and values?

- How does your group communicate its progress in those areas?

Empowerment

Encourage risk-taking with reflection and accountability

An empowered leader takes risks and encourages all team members to do the same with reflection and accountability. Staying progressive and competitive in today's global business setting requires nothing less. Some leadership practices are cyclical. An empowering leader will recognize the things that work. It's the role of the leader to ensure the organization doesn't go back in time but moves forward, building upon identified effective practices and incorporating new research and learning along the way.

Empowering people to be progressive while staying focused on the agreed-upon visions and goals will produce desired outcomes—perhaps achieved in new, exciting ways. It is essential for leaders to "try on" new initiatives even though it may take them or the people they work with out of their comfort zone. Exploring alternatives to existing ideas, plans, and initiatives will help to keep your organization competitive. Support, don't suppress, ideas that may challenge the status quo.

Encourage forward thinking by empowering your team to think outside the box–this sends a message of trust and a belief that together you can make a difference. "Out of the box" thinking gives people a chance to share their creative and innovative ideas. It also challenges the status quo and can help break the cycle of mediocrity. Thinking outside the box sparks initiative. Empowering leaders embrace out of the box thinking, model it, and encourage it from those they lead.

Risk-taking and out of the box thinking need collective buy-in and monitoring. An empowering leader will facilitate new initiatives and provide unconditional support through reflection and accountability. Reflection is done through consistent communication and dialogue with and among the people who are leading the work. In small groups, or one-on-one, reflection based on data needs to be common practice. Questions of what worked, what didn't, need to be addressed collaboratively. Use my four "R's" as a guide. . . Revisit, Reflect, Revise, Re-energize until desired outcomes are achieved. This is part of the monitoring process which includes careful analysis, evaluation, and accountability. The leader who empowers has created a culture of trust and uses that trust to guide the accountability process. Monitoring can be daily, weekly, or monthly. It's important to stay current and consistent with the "check-in" process. Collaborate on a reflection and accountability plan that will ensure timelines and results are met.

Gentle Reminder:

Leaders who are not empowered themselves cannot encourage or empower risk-taking from their team members.

Reflections:

- What stands in the way of risk-taking?

- What are some downfalls and pitfalls of risk-taking and how can they be avoided?

- How can you learn from risk-taking gone bad?

- How do trust and expertise factor into risk-taking?

- What's the biggest professional risk you have ever taken? What would you do differently?

- Does your environment reflect your visions, goals, beliefs?

- What system do you have in place to ensure initiatives are working?

- How will you address the process of the four "R's"?

- How do you monitor results and accountability?

Create an environment where people want to participate with full hearts

You've got to love your people more than your position. ~Anonymous

The real wisdom is out in the field. ~Colin Powell

People matter regardless of the capacity in which they serve an organization. Creating an environment where people want to participate with full hearts can increase productivity and desired results. When people feel they have something to contribute and they know their contributions are valued, they become energized. An empowering leader identifies expertise in the workplace through observation, conversations, and results, and assigns tasks accordingly.

It is imperative that you trust, value, and acknowledge expertise and contributions. Trust is essential for creating an empowered workplace grounded in respect and professional courtesy. Trust is part of relationship-building and creates a non-threatening culture where appreciation for a job well done is obvious. When you lead with heart, trust is created and opens doors for people to work together in the best interests of their organization, instead of promoting personal and/or political agendas. Trusting the expertise of the people around you leads to people feeling motivated to explore, dream, and discover!

When building a culture of trust in the workplace, empowering leaders make an effort to reduce, and ideally eliminate, the practice of "micro-managing". An empowered leader trusts, believes, and promotes the expertise that exists within an organization. When people feel trusted and supported, they are happy and willing to put forth extra efforts to become better at their craft.

An empowering leader identifies differences and capitalizes on strengths by creating an environment that recognizes, utilizes, and balances the team's expertise. People are empowered when a leader capitalizes on that wisdom to drive the work.

We all work harder when we think we are appreciated and valued for our knowledge, skills, and performance. Empowering leaders show that they value the work being done by taking the time to utilize and acknowledge the expertise around them. It puts people in the mindset that they are respected and work in an environment that appreciates what they have to offer.

Encouraging and expecting collegial respect and teamwork creates an environment that makes the most of individual talents and capabilities. This kind of an environment energizes people to develop the confidence they need to give their personal best every day and recognizes their contributions.

Feeding inner energy and promoting self-worth through heart-healthy leadership will increase a group's productivity… not because it is an expectation but because people feel part of the team and therefore participate with full hearts. We can't force people to work to their potential but we can create an environment where they *want* to work to their potential.

Collaboration and synergy are key to a successful partnership. People who see that their ideas and suggestions are valued and implemented feel empowered to give more. Collaboration encourages all members to contribute in ways that not only increase productivity but enhance the work environment as well. Having an absolute and collective allegiance to the beliefs, visions, and goals set by you and your team sets the tone for an environment fueled by synergy. Collaboration creates synergy which grows from an unconditional commitment of the team that respects each member's talents and expertise as it relates to the task at hand. Making the practice of collaboration public will send a unified message of an organization grounded in common core values and beliefs with the talent, experience, and commitment to get the job done with excellence.

You can't do it alone…the big picture is a very inclusive landscape. Synergy plays a key role in the process of establishing partnerships among stakeholders that empower and inspire excellence. Elements of a synergized work environment are collaboration…teamwork…partnership…cooperation…commonalities. Part of creating a synergized work environment is knowing and trusting the experience and expertise of your staff. It also includes knowing how to tap into the best and brightest to contribute to the success of a project or achievement of a goal. A leader with heart is inclusive, not exclusive, and is the one who opens the door to opportunities and possibilities.

Developing a collaborative and synergized partnership among the people you lead is a key component to achieving goals and objectives.

Gentle Reminders:

Valuing coworkers is an essential part of showing respect and building confidence.

Leaders who dictate or micro-manage demonstrate a lack of trust and may affect surface change only.

Trust facilitates higher productivity.

Empowerment

Reflections:

- Does upper management show they value your contributions to the organization? If so, in what ways?

- How do you express value?

- How do your team members express value?

- How does your organization make time for collaboration?

- Does your team sit at a round table to encourage collaboration or at a rectangular table with you at the head?

- Who are the leaders of leaders within your organization?

- How do you demonstrate trust in your workplace?

- How do you create an atmosphere of trust?

- How do you, as a leader, model trust for your team members?

- Do you trust YOUR leaders? Why?

- How do you inspire those you lead?

- What do you do when trust is breached or compromised? How does that affect your workplace?

- What did you do today to create synergy in your environment?

- How do you build teams with synergy in mind?

- How do you empower synergy?

- Can synergy be measured?

- List your core beliefs about:

    - Building relationships in the workplace

    - Team work

Keep an open heart, open mind…open door

Always keep an open mind and a compassionate heart. ~Phil Jackson

Minds are like parachutes—they only function when they are open.
~Thomas Dewar

Empowering leaders will have an open heart, open mind, open door policy. They support team members' thinking, ideas, and suggestions by listening and encouraging with an open mind. When there is an open door policy, people generally feel comfortable sharing their thoughts and ideas in support of continuous improvement.

Leaders with an open heart take time to listen, gather information, and analyze needs to ensure effective, meaningful, and quality management/support systems reach all team members. There is so much untapped creativity in the workplace. Let encouragement of creativity, ideas, and suggestions from the people around you be an integral part of your leadership style.

Keep your heart and mind open to innovation and creativity. Create an environment that promotes a sense of collective energy by being positive, having a sense of purpose and vision, having a full sense of self, being aware of your role as a creator and nurturer, and engaging in the moment with a full heart. Facilitate greatness, don't dictate it….

Gentle Reminder:

An open door DOES give the impression of an open mind.

Empowerment

Reflections:

- How do you encourage new ideas?

- How do you acknowledge that those who are doing the work probably know more about some aspects of the work than you do?

- How do you invite constructive change?

- Do you have "open door" hours when anyone is welcome to speak with you?

Celebrate the work dance

Dancing with the feet is one thing, but dancing with the heart is another.
~Anonymous

You can dance anywhere, even if only in your heart. ~Unknown

Celebrating the work dance means to respect and capitalize on the fact that everyone has life stories and even genetic dispositions that influence their decision making skills and attitudes towards the workplace. Howard Gardner's Theory of Multiple Intelligences offers the concept that we learn and have skill sets developed using our individual intellectual strengths. Your team has unique talents and accesses knowledge using different modalities. It's up to you as the leader with heart to provide an environment that promotes such individuality.

Applying the concept of the work dance means that if a person needs to work with music in the background, then let it be. If a person needs to have a colorful work space, then let it be. If a person wishes to move around while thinking and planning, then let it be. Some people take notes using technology while others use outlines or color and pictures. Celebrate and respectfully acknowledge the uniqueness of personalities and avenues people take to get the job done. Productivity goes up when people are in a comfort zone that they helped to create. If you put people in the right environment, they will thrive!

Gentle Reminder:

People learn in different ways. Some learn best by reading, others by seeing and having a concept demonstrated, others by hearing an explanation. Often, it is the combination of many modes of communication that results in the highest level of understanding.

Reflections:

- What single past experience strongly influences your work life?

- If a person needs music to do their work, how does that affect others in proximity?

- To what extent do you allow people to create their own "comfort zone"?

- What do you do when one person's comfort zone conflicts with that of another?

- How do you express your own comfort zone?

Celebrate and appreciate

Appreciation is a wonderful thing. It makes what is excellent in others belong to us as well. ~Voltaire

We must never forget that the highest appreciation is not to utter words, but to live by them. ~J.F. Kennedy

The deepest principle in human nature is the craving to be appreciated.
~William James

Appreciation can make a day, even change a life. Your willingness to put it into words is all that is necessary. ~Margaret Cousins

Appreciation and acknowledgement of team efforts and a job well done build a stronger community. Appreciation can be as simple as affirming through warm eye contact, a smile, thumbs up, or verbal congratulations when a team member has excelled or accomplished a task. The same goes for recognizing a team member who has put forth effort toward achieving a goal. People like to be cheered along—keep the energy and momentum going by keeping praise in your daily communication.

Acknowledge efforts and accomplishments on a daily basis and people will respond—it's only human. We all enjoy a pat on the back once in a while. An empowered leader will develop a fair and equitable system for acknowledging talent, ideas, creativity, and success. When people feel valued, they work harder and smarter. An empowered leader can acknowledge the talents and accomplishments by a simple thank you, written announcement in a weekly or monthly newsletter, or acknowledgement at a staff meeting. Empowering people to do their personal best can be accomplished by personally showing that you appreciate, trust, and honor their work—this is the heart of the work. Taking the time to honor the experts in the field leads to a synergized environment where people want to come together to achieve results.

It takes a leader who leads with heart and has confidence without arrogance to acknowledge where an idea or result came from. Giving credit to the movers and shakers shows unconditional support for innovation and creativity. It provides for a heart-healthy work environment where people feel confident and safe to create, innovate, and share with trust in their heart.

Part of building a culture of trust and recognition is to give credit where credit is due. An empowered leader will honor everyone's creativity. Many leaders today tend to have their own personal agendas and desires for personal promotional growth, therefore taking sole credit for results. An empowering leader will go public with success stories, paying tribute to the great minds behind it. People will continue to excel if they continue to be honored for their accomplishments. It is human nature to want praise and recognition for our work. Giving credit where credit is due is part of the nurturing process of the heart.

One of the most empowering tools a leader can use to promote a heart-healthy workplace is to initiate praise and appreciation with the heart as the guide. Your colleagues deserve to be acknowledged for their accomplishments. Empowering leaders encourage, model, and promote individual potential and success through appreciation, acknowledgement, honesty, respect, and heart. The feeling of being appreciated is one of the greatest feelings in the human spirit, it's the job of the leader to nurture that feeling.

Gentle Reminder:

People can never be thanked too much.

Reflections:

- Think about the times when someone complimented your work. Think about how it made you feel when you realized someone took note and showed appreciation to you, as a contributing member of the workplace.

- How is your work acknowledged? Why is it important?

- What methods do you use to acknowledge good work?

- What benefits have you seen from acknowledging excellence in the workplace?

- What are some examples of your personal best?

- What are some examples of personal best from your staff?

- Are you careful to acknowledge everyone and not just a few stars?

- Who did you thank/recognize today and why? This week? This month?

- Can you list the innovations, ideas, and strategies in place that have produced results? Can you list the names of the people who generated these things? How did you acknowledge these people?

Empowerment

> Character is doing the right thing when nobody's looking. There are too many people who think that the only thing that's right is to get by and the only thing that's wrong is to get caught. ~J.C. Watts

character

> Character is higher than intellect.
> ~Ralph Waldo Emerson

> Character is not about living up to the expectations of others, its about living up to the expectations you have for yourself.
> ~Laurie Hinzman

Character is the life skill used to achieve success in your personal and professional life. It is the values and beliefs that exist within you and make impressions on others—consciously or subconsciously. Character is demonstrated by how you live your life. It is individualized, begins the moment you are born, and evolves throughout your lifetime. It represents your moral values and ethical standards in your approach to life. How you develop and refine your character is your personal responsibility.

The heart is the center of your emotions . . .your actions are driven and influenced by emotions . . . it is through your actions that you portray your true character. How you respond to situations and interact with others is a direct reflection of who you are and what you value. Character is influenced by the heart; it is your job to ensure your heart is in the right place.

Character defines who you are and plays an intrinsic role on how you treat and work with others. Character influences the implementation of work, the "how" of the work. It takes quality and heartfelt character to create a work environment that is non-threatening and supportive. Your character will influence the work ethic, morale and productivity of the people you lead.

The list of human characteristics is long; however, there are some key features and traits that define the qualities needed in support of heart healthy leadership:

- Attitude
- Honesty
- Courage
- Perseverance
- Respect
- Giving

Attitude

Positive attitudes will succeed! ~Laurie Hinzman

Attitude is a little thing that makes a big difference. ~Winston Churchill

Attitude is about character. A heart-healthy attitude, simply stated, is about having a positive outlook on life. A positive attitude will lead to happiness, good health, and success. Your attitude towards the work, the successes, the defeats, and the challenges will be the guiding force for everyone else's attitude. When things are going great, create and join in on the celebrations—when things are not going well use my four "R's"—revisit, reflect, revise, and re-energize! Your dispositions and mannerisms are contagious . . . as a leader you are not allowed to have a bad day. If you do, think of a way to keep it from spreading (going public). Find a way to adjust your attitude in the face of those you lead. When the chips are down, find a colleague or friend who can help redirect your energies into a positive zone. When presented with a negative outlook or statement, rephrase the statement into a positive one. Help others to see the light at the end of the tunnel. When there is a systemic negative attitude—low morale among colleagues—make sure you do not take on the attitude of others. Remain in touch with your own feelings that keep your attitude in check. Your attitude matters.

A positive, happy, healthy attitude is good for your body, mind and soul... it reduces stress. When your attitude becomes bad it negatively impacts your work which negatively impacts the work of others. If the system is getting you down, do an attitude adjustment. If you allow the system to break you, then you have given too much power to the system. My father used to tell me that when the going gets tough the tough get going. When work-related stress overwhelmed me, he would encourage me to take time to write down the positives and negatives of my job (or what's affecting my attitude). This practice will help you figure out (compartmentalize) what is making your attitude negative. Come to terms with it—then you can adjust your attitude accordingly. When you adjust and move it back into the positive zone, you are going to see and feel results. Your overall health will be better and stress levels reduced.

Gentle Reminders:

Your positive attitude will encourage and inspire the positive attitude of others.

Those who influence the hearts and minds of others are not allowed to have a bad day . . . keep your attitude heart-healthy and the heart health of others will follow.

Reflections:

- Is your professional attitude healthy?

- What factors in your life influence your attitude?

- What factors in your business influence your attitude?

- Does the majority of your staff have a positive attitude?

- How do you address negative attitudes in your organization?

Honesty

Honest hearts produce honest actions. ~Brigham Young

Honesty is the cornerstone of all success, without which confidence and ability to perform shall cease to exist. ~Mary Kay Ash

People who are dishonest have a hard time remembering their web of lies. ~Robert Hinzman

Honesty is the character trait that keeps your spirit morally and ethically strong. Honesty represents the positive attributes of honor, integrity, trustworthiness, and dignity. It is an unselfish and sincere characteristic that promotes trust within any organization. Building relationships grounded in honesty gives the leader credibility and respect. When a leader is honest they will gain the trust and confidence of the people they lead and vice-versa. Honesty serves as a model for what you expect within the organization.

Honesty is about reality . . . facing the facts and seeing things for what they truly are. When telling the truth, one doesn't have to worry about what will be said down the road. It's always easier to remember what really happened versus something that was made up to cover the truth. Dishonesty creates a road with multiple paths and turns—people who go down this road will have a hard time reaching their destination.

Honesty is having the ability to be trustworthy. The people you lead need to know that they can talk to you in confidence and know their words, thinking, or ideas will go no further. Your team needs to know that what is said in confidence stays in confidence. They need to be able to trust you with their fears and challenges and that you will be their confidant. Together with honesty and trustworthiness, confidentiality plays an incredible role in building positive and heart-healthy relationships.

Confidentiality is the ability to keep the secrets of others. When someone entrusts you with secrets then you must honor that trust by keeping the secret confidential. Sometimes situations arise that may test your ability to keep the secret. The ability to be one hundred percent honest can be influenced by the situation. Will the truth betray someone who has put their trust in you? Your professional responsibility is to honor confidentiality, especially if it is in the best interest of the organization. When confronted with questions that might jeopardize confidential information, the best practice is to be honest and say – "it's confidential".

Gossip and rumor mills start by people betraying one another's confidence, leading to a deficit of trust within the organization. People need to know that their workplace is safe and free from gossip. People need to be able to trust their leader and in turn, you as the leader, need to trust those you lead. Being trustworthy means that you will do what you say you're going to do, you will follow through on things you say you will, you will follow policy and procedures, and you will be fair. Trustworthiness goes both ways—when you keep your standards grounded in honesty and trustworthiness then those you lead are expected to do the same. They need to know that you will be trustworthy and you expect the same from them, unconditionally.

> **Gentle Reminder:**
>
> Honesty is a character trait that represents integrity, high morals, values, trustworthiness, and class. Take to heart what someone once told me: "Do not repeat anything you will not sign your name to."

Reflections:

- Do you feel you have honest and open communication with your staff? What are your methods of communication?

- When communicating to stakeholders are you honest about the realities the organization is faced with?

- Have you been in a situation where honesty was hurtful? Did it impact one person, several, or the greater good?

- Have you been asked, or required by a superior, to keep a secret that could potentially harm the morale or efficacy of your organization? What was the circumstance and what steps did you take to ensure the organization maintained its integrity?

- Define what a secret means.

- Are you trustworthy?

- Do you trust your team to be confidential when asked?

Courage

The key to change is to let go of fear. ~Rosanne Cash

If my mind can conceive it and my heart can believe it, I know I can achieve it. ~Jesse Jackson

Courage is what it takes to stand up and speak; courage is also what it takes to sit down and listen. ~Winston Churchill

Courage is the ability to face situations without fear. Leading with the heart as a guide is a courageous act energized by an unconditional commitment to people and results. Courage is knowing and pursuing what is right and rejecting what is wrong. It is a trait that influences and impacts change and progress within any organization. Courage comes from within and gains strength through personal and professional experiences. Courage is about believing that you can and will accomplish what needs to be done despite antagonism and criticism. When faced with adversity, fear surfaces—how much power you give that fear is up to you.

Courage cannot be granted, it must be developed. The ability to look fear in the face with confidence will give you the courage to move forward. Surviving difficult times that challenge the heart will fuel courage. Courage will become stronger the more you face failure with a full heart and embrace a willingness to learn and try again. Courage is about having the guts to stick it out.

Creating new visions and goals that move people out of their comfort zones takes courage. Setting and initiating new standards of excellence which promote productivity and success within an organization takes courage. Initiating change is an act of courage sustained by your passion and belief that you are smart enough to get through the toughest of times. Trust your heart, believe that you can overcome fear and courage will follow.

Gentle Reminder:

Courage is something that grows with experience through the ability to confront fear with confidence and perseverance.

Reflections:

- When you initiated change within your organization, what kind of obstacles did you face? How did you resolve (dissolve) the obstacles?

- What are your greatest fears within your profession?

- When confronted with unfounded criticism or attacks on your character, do you have the courage to take steps to right the wrong?

- What are some situations that provoked fear in you? How did you handle them? How would you handle it differently—or would you?

- Define courage. Do you consider yourself to be a courageous leader?

- Who is your ally when you need someone to help you address fears/challenges in leadership? How does this person support you?

Perseverance

Nobody trips over mountains. It is the small pebble that causes you to stumble. Pass all the pebbles in your path and you will find you have crossed the mountain. ~Author Unknown

Ride out the storm—for it too shall pass. ~Laurie Hinzman

The difference between perseverance and obstinacy is that one comes from a strong will, and the other from a strong won't. ~Henry Ward Beecher

Don't be afraid to give your best to what seemingly are small jobs. Every time you conquer one it makes you that much stronger. If you do the little jobs well, the big ones will tend to take care of themselves. ~Dale Carnegie

It takes courage to initiate change. With that courage comes an unconditional commitment to getting the job done despite difficulties, obstacles, or discouragement. A leader with heart will model and collaborate with perseverance and determination as the driving force to achieve success within the organization. Perseverance is about dedication and passion and needs the support of the people who work with you. Perseverance is about being persistent, with heart, and not at the expense of others. Your attitude must exemplify the message that you will not give up, nor do you expect your people to give up, despite what others may wish for you. Stay focused and determined to promote success and achieve goals.

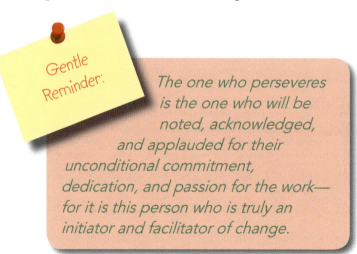

Gentle Reminder: The one who perseveres is the one who will be noted, acknowledged, and applauded for their unconditional commitment, dedication, and passion for the work—for it is this person who is truly an initiator and facilitator of change.

Reflections:

- What was one of the biggest obstacles you have faced in your profession?

- Have you ever abandoned an idea you felt would produce positive results? Why?

- What is something you are striving for at this time? How long have you been working toward it? Has it taken you longer than expected? What obstacles are in your way?

Character

Respect

Respect is an unselfish feeling that is absent of threat, resentment, and jealousy. ~Laurie Hinzman

Respect feeds innovation and creativity. ~Laurie Hinzman

Respect your efforts, respect yourself. Self-respect leads to self-discipline. When you have both firmly under your belt, that's real power. ~Clint Eastwood

If you want to be respected by others the great thing is to respect yourself. Only by that, only by self-respect will you compel others to respect you.
~Fyodor Dostoyevsky

Today's society requires an increased level of understanding in the importance of respect. The act of showing respect to one another regardless of age, race, gender, talent, or position has lost its appeal and importance in society. Maybe people's lives are so busy and fast-paced that they don't take the time to notice the people around them or when they themselves are being rude or disrespectful because they are in a hurry or inconvenienced. Showing respect and consideration to others is an honorable trait that I was brought up with. It was an expectation not an exception in my family. Respect comes from the heart and plays an empowering role in relationship building.

To disrespect is heartless, while treating others the way you wish to be treated is a model that exemplifies honor. A respectful person is one who gives respect to others. The practice of giving respect will in turn earn a person respect which supports the notion of "what goes around comes around". The ability to be respectful, no matter your position, shows true unselfish character.

People feel good about themselves when they feel appreciated; however, it should not be a one-way street. Mutual respect is the ability to collectively:

- Show appreciation for one another's talents and contributions to the organization
- Acknowledge one another for intellect, knowledge, and skills that support and promote excellence regardless of position
- Show gratitude and appreciation for someone's efforts

- Acknowledge individuality and uniqueness of personalities
- Honor people's time
- Support one another in failure and challenging times

Regardless of your rank, position, or title, it is your moral and ethical responsibility to be respectful and courteous towards the people you lead. Holding a position of power doesn't give a leader the right to engage in put-downs and disrespect. A person in a position of power has tough decisions to make every day, but not at the expense of others. Regardless of the situation, all decisions should be handled with dignity and respect. When a leader treats people honorably and respectfully, it is a tribute to who they are as a person. People may not be equal when it comes to positions of power; however, they are equal when it comes to how they are to be treated in a professional setting. A leader with heart will make it common practice to show respect and fairness to everyone. Showing appreciation and gratitude for commitment and dedication will increase productivity, efficacy, and results. When people feel appreciated they will come to work with full hearts ready to problem-solve and give their personal best.

Honoring chain of command is another professional obligation of a leader with heart. Honoring the position and title of the person or people above you is about respect, unconditionally. When things are going smoothly, honoring the chain is easy; however, when the relationship between you and your immediate supervisor gets rough, the heart is challenged. When there is disagreement between your supervisor and you, a show of respect is expected—even if you don't feel it. When receiving feedback from your supervisor, take it professionally and respectfully, even if you don't agree with it. Don't burn a bridge, don't lash out emotionally, over-react, or be unprofessional, as you never know when your paths may cross again.

If you are unhappy with your relationship with your supervisor, identify what the problem is, face it with confidence and integrity, and have the courage to do something about it, respectfully. Keep respect in your tone and communication (written and verbal) when working with your superior—you would expect nothing less from those you lead. Try to resolve the issue with them as the initial step—if things don't change, then consider next steps keeping the heart, professionalism, truth, and respect as your guide. Honoring and respecting the chain of command is the right thing to do. Agree, in your heart, to disagree respectfully—but never compromise your integrity.

Gentle Reminder:

In the end, we are all separate: our stories, no matter how similar, come to a fork and diverge. We are drawn to each other because of our similarities, but we must learn to respect our differences.

Reflections:

- Have you ever had a disagreement with your supervisor where you felt you had to go above their head? What steps did you take? What was the outcome? What would you do differently if you had the chance?

- How do you show respect to the people you work with?

- In what ways do people show/give you respect?

- Is there ever a time for a supervisor to treat people disrespectfully? Why or why not?

Giving

Leadership from the heart requires the unconditional and unselfish giving of your time, heart, and mind. When you have nothing more to give or start to resent the giving, it's time for a "you" check. ~Laurie Hinzman

You give but little when you give of your possessions. It is when you give of yourself that you truly give. ~Kahlil Gibran

The first step to leadership is servanthood. ~John Maxwell

In any relationship, it is better to give than receive. Examples of giving are:

- Giving credit vs. taking credit
- Giving praise vs. expecting praise
- Saying thank you vs. expecting to be thanked
- Giving of your time vs. taking the time of others

Effective leaders will spend the majority of their days coaching, listening, planning collaboratively, guiding, supporting, facilitating, etc. in support of the needs of the organization. There is very little down time, very little, if any, "me" time. An effective, inspiring, and motivating leader will spend the whole work day giving . . . it's the heart of leadership. The higher you climb in an organization, the more you have to give of yourself to others. To expect the same in return from those you lead is unreasonable and unrealistic. Leadership is about giving, giving from the heart, whether you have the time or not. The unselfish giving of your time, heart, mind, and expertise is what makes you a credible and respected leader.

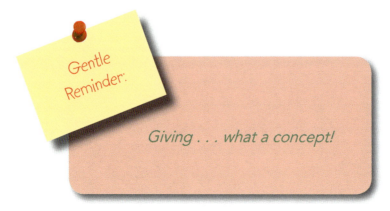

Gentle Reminder:

Giving . . . what a concept!

Reflections:

- How much of your giving time is devoted to personnel issues?

- How much of your time is devoted to the real work of your business?

- Document your days for a week and determine how much time is devoted to paperwork vs. active engagement in planning with your team.

> Staying true to your own core values and beliefs is a matter of the heart and an honest testament of your own moral and ethical character, it's called integrity. Leading with integrity is heart-healthy leadership.
> ~Laurie Hinzman

integrity

> Just being honest is not enough. The essential ingredient is executive integrity. ~Philip Crosby

> I cannot find language of sufficient energy to convey my sense of the sacredness of private integrity. ~Ralph Waldo Emerson

> Be who you are and say what you feel because those who mind don't matter and those who matter don't mind.
> ~Dr. X

Integrity is part of a person's overall character. I think it's such an important element of leading with heart that I dedicated a chapter to it. Integrity relates to our ethical value system and the consistency with which we apply it in our day-to-day living and leading. It is the essence of our being, the foundation of dignity, grace, honor, respect, and heart. Without integrity we set ourselves up for confusion, distraction, disappointments, and frustration. Without integrity, we really have nothing.

Integrity is the uncompromising adherence to moral and ethical principles; soundness of moral character, honesty; the state of being whole or entire. Integrity is about honor and honesty with yourself and others.

Integrity is a profound concept often used loosely when describing character. It means simply "to do the right thing without hurting others". The misuse or overuse of this honorable word comes when people have a difference of opinion as to what the right thing is.

You've heard that "knowledge is power". Like knowledge, integrity is both powerful and empowering when it becomes the heart of your work.

Integrity is one of the cornerstones of leading with heart. Strong, effective, and empowering leadership is grounded in moral and ethical values. When you lead with integrity, you:

- Stay true to the heart of the work
- Never compromise your integrity
- Make an absolute and unconditional commitment
- Advocate equity and fairness
- Promote with integrity
- Practice transparency
- Recognize when it is time to move on

Stay true to the heart of the work

Have the courage to say no. Have the courage to face the truth. Do the right thing because it is right. These are the magic keys to living your life with integrity. ~W. Clement Stone

Many actions and reactions are driven by politics, individual needs or wants, greed, and/or trends. A leader who leads with integrity will have the courage to initiate internal changes based on needs identified jointly with their team. Integrity can be challenged when there are outside influences, opinions, and directives that differ from what you know to be best for your team. When challenged, revisit the purpose and goals of your work, they are the "heart of the work".

Staying true to the heart of the work, regardless of challenges and barriers, will ensure expected outcomes can be achieved. A leader who leads with integrity will stay focused on the heart of the work regardless of negative influences. A leader with integrity will take directives from above and adapt them to support the real work within their organization. Staying true to the heart of the work means a leader will use shared vision and collaborative goal setting (Empowerment chapter) as an unconditional guide, staying focused on what matters most—results.

> **Gentle Reminder:**
>
> *Working with integrity makes the job easier, and often, more fun. Honesty and integrity are essential components of heart-healthy leadership.*

Reflections:

- Write your definition of integrity—what does integrity mean to you?

- How do you model integrity in the workplace?

- Give an example that demonstrates the integrity of your organization.

- Do your systems have integrity? How is that demonstrated?

- Did your decisions and actions today truly reflect what you believe and value?

- Have you ever had to defend the work you and your staff have successfully implemented? What was the circumstance and outcome? How did (do) you feel about the experience—what leadership lessons did you learn?

- What are your core beliefs about using integrity to guide your leadership practice?

Never compromise your integrity

The higher you climb the mountain the stronger the wind. ~Anonymous

Living the truth in your heart without compromise brings kindness into the world. Attempts at kindness that compromise your heart cause only sadness. ~Anonymous

It's true that the systematic and political stresses of the workplace can press us to bend our integrity, but it's our responsibility as leaders to ensure the stresses don't negate our fundamental values. Some leaders compromise their core beliefs to stay in good graces with their superior for fear of losing their job. This behavior is often found in a work environment where a top-down management style prevails. It is often characterized by intimidation and fear-driven communications. Leaders who adopt this management style are more dictator than facilitator; they do not incorporate the heart into their leadership practice.

Stay above the political agendas that drive leaders to treat people disrespectfully. By following your heart and sticking to your morals you will end up on top and be the one who truly makes the difference!

Take suggestions and feedback with an open mind, then deliver and implement in a style that does not compromise your integrity. We can all improve upon the work we are doing, but compromising the heart work and our integrity when initiating change could create a work environment that is "non-synergized".

Gentle Reminder:

To compromise your integrity to support the political and personal agendas of others is to compromise your own core beliefs and values... follow your heart because it will make the difference.

Reflections:

- Has there been a time when you were asked to compromise your integrity on the job? How did you handle it?

- List some benefits of working with integrity.

- Are you doing the work the way someone has told you to or are you leading the work the way you and your team have agreed to accomplish the work?

- Have you had to compromise your integrity to support directives, personal, or political agendas? When and what were the results?

- What are your frustrations? Obstacles? How do they relate to leading with integrity?

Make an absolute and unconditional commitment

Integrity is what we do, what we say, and what we say we do. ~Don Galer

Your absolute and unconditional commitment as a leader with integrity is an essential element into your organization's success. Effective leadership involves a pledge and commitment from your heart to give unconditionally the time, energy, and focus to the work for which you are responsible. A leader who leads with integrity will work for the good of the organization, its people, and expected outcomes. It takes confidence, courage, and integrity to keep your heart in the work. Stay focused and committed with a full heart or make plans to move on.

Outside pressures and influences can harm or negatively impact the progress and ultimate success of the work. It is natural and appropriate for a leader to protect the team from those. In fact, leading for continuous improvement requires leaders to compartmentalize those stresses and pressures, to separate the pressures that can help the work from those with the potential to put it at risk. Filtering stress can cause people internal stress and potentially cast a shadow of doubt on your own commitment to the work. Eventually it will reflect in your leadership. It is key to remember who you are (without arrogance) and why you are in your job. When stress starts to impact your own confidence or commitment to the work, remember to implement my four "R's" by taking time to <u>revisit</u> the reasons for the work and its success. <u>Reflect</u> on the strategies you facilitated to get there as well as your own core beliefs, and if appropriate, <u>revise</u> and <u>re-energize</u> your attitude and approach to the work.

If the stresses of life are getting in the way of your performance and heart commitment then you need to rethink what you are doing or adjust your attitude towards the work so you can refocus your attention with 100% commitment. Protect your heart, the heart of others, and the heart of the work by continuing to move forward with what you know best regardless of what's going on around you. Fight for what you believe in with commitment, passion, and integrity.

Gentle Reminder:

Absolute commitment helps you focus on the tasks to be done.

Reflections:

- Do you have an absolute and unconditional commitment to the work?

- What does unconditional commitment mean to you?

- Do you have a full heart for the work you are doing and the work you expect your teams to do?

- How does absolute commitment relate to integrity on the job?

- Are you able to compartmentalize stress or is it consuming you to the point where you are questioning your own leadership style, vision, and goals? Identify where the stress is coming from.

- Create a chart that compartmentalizes your stress.

- When is it time to revisit, reflect, revise, and re-energize?

- Do you have total buy-in from upper management and from your team for the work you are doing? Do you believe in what you are doing?

Advocate equity and fairness

Fairness is not an attitude. It's a professional skill that must be developed and exercised. ~Brit Hume

Integrity is all about treating people equitably and fairly. When setting policies and procedures, a leader with heart makes sure the guidelines are equitable and fair to the entire team. When setting expectations and making decisions, make sure the standards set are the same for everyone.

Being fair means you are not biased, dishonest, or creating injustices. Being fair sends a clear message from the heart that all members are treated as equals when it comes to accountability and work ethic. When mixed practices come into play, the work environment can become toxic and threatening. Double standards are common practice in some workplaces due to friendships and "who you know" practices. Don't let that be part of your leadership style. Fairness, equity, and integrity matter.

Gentle Reminder:

Fairness is what gives order to your world.

Reflections:

- Do you periodically review your standards, policies, procedures, and practices to assure they are fair and equitable?

- How do you assure that you treat everyone fairly?

- What can happen when a leader shows bias toward a person...a project?

Promote with integrity

A leader with integrity does not compromise that integrity to promote a friend over someone more qualified for a position. Sadly, promotion based on "who you know" is a well-known practice.

In addition to incompetent friends of the boss being promoted, the "The Peter Principle" (*The Peter Principle*, Laurence J. Peter, 1969), or "Petrina Principle" as women like to say, is a practice where men or women are promoted beyond their level of competence because of someone they know or because they are people pleasers. Mr. Peter refers to the injustices of promoting people to their level of incompetence in his book and states, "The incompetent with nothing to do can still make a mess of it." In his research, he found "occupational incompetence was everywhere".

A leader with integrity does not compromise professional relationships for a friendship in the workplace. Using friendship as a guide for promotion or recognition will do irreversible damage to the morale of your colleagues. Using the Peter Principle as a leadership practice will cause anger, discontent, mistrust, and low morale.

A leader with integrity will promote based on performance combined with character and ethical standards. You must have honor and discipline to build your team, promote based on merit, and stay focused and true to your integrity.

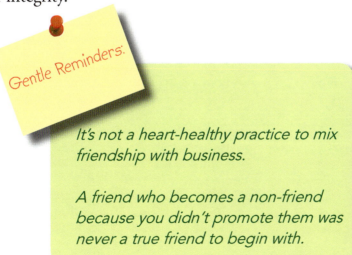

Gentle Reminders:

It's not a heart-healthy practice to mix friendship with business.

A friend who becomes a non-friend because you didn't promote them was never a true friend to begin with.

Integrity

Reflections:

- Have you observed the Peter Principle in action in your organization?

- What's the difference between a friend and a trusted colleague?

- Have you promoted, recognized, and/or done favors for someone because they are your friend, possibly overlooking another who may out- perform your friend?

- Have you been a victim of this practice?

- What steps do you have in place to ensure promotions are based on performance, integrity, and ethics?

Practice transparency

Being transparent is part of building synergy. ~Laurie Hinzman

Transparency is an important element of integrity. It entails being open and honest about the realities of the organization. Part of building relationships is to be transparent through consistent and open communication. Building a climate of trust comes from the leader who is willing to share successes, challenges, and defeats, without compromising confidentiality, in a non-threatening but professional manner. When you and your team hold transparency as a fundamental ethic, it can operate more efficiently. Be consistently open and honest about status, standards, and practices of the organization.

Gentle Reminder:

Transparency and accountability require integrity.

Reflections:

- How are transparency and integrity related?

- How does transparency cut down on gossip and time wasted by speculating?

- How does transparency build trusting relationships?

- Are the leaders in your organization open to transparent communication?

- Do your employees know the ups and downs of the organization or do you tend to shield them from knowing?

- When is it appropriate to keep secrets from your group?

Recognize when it's time to move on

Declare victory and quit. Command is lonely, so is the decision to withdraw from authority. ~Colin Powell

A true and effective leader with integrity puts heart and soul into the work. But consistently implementing the heart work is tough when those around you don't bring the same level of commitment, dedication, experience, and skill. Bureaucratic systems or poor leadership in upper management can prevent you from being effective and efficient and prevent you from achieving your personal best, which can lead to "burn out".

It's important to take time to look within your heart and evaluate your own feelings. A leader who leads with integrity will constantly touch base with their inner self and determine next steps. An unsettled or unhappy leader cannot empower through synergy or other means if their heart isn't fully engaged. A "one foot out the door" mindset will lead to your team's fragmentation and your inability to lead the work effectively.

The heart matters, so when you no longer feel the challenge or satisfaction, or the excitement and passion to get the job done...when you no longer believe in the relevance of the work or the probability that the goal can be accomplished—ever, it may be time to make a change... for you.

Take responsibility for your own professional growth. Making a career or job classification change is a challenging decision. Having the heart to admit you have done all you can to promote organizational health and success is a tribute to your integrity. Recognizing you no longer have the heart to facilitate continuous growth at the level where you are is the first step to moving on. Stay true to the work at hand but begin networking with colleagues and friends to explore new options for your sake as well as for the sake of the organization.

Gentle Reminder:

Many people have three or more different careers in a lifetime.

Integrity

Reflections:

- Is your job still challenging to you? If yes, in what ways? If no, why?

- Is your heart divided between now and next steps?

- Where do you see yourself in a year, in five years?

- Imagine the ideal leadership position that suits your talents, experience, and integrity.

Integrity

voice

What you say and do is a reflection of who you are and gives permission to others to say and do the same. *~Laurie Hinzman*

Communication leads to community, that is, to understanding, intimacy and mutual valuing. *~Rollo May*

Voice is part of the leader's heart work repertoire; it represents verbal and non-verbal expressions that articulate character or quality in any given moment. It's about self-expression and the ability to proclaim and declare core beliefs and standards by which you live. Voicing with heart sets the avenue through which opinions, choices, and desires are expressed. It is the path through which the views of leaders and team members are expressed.

Speaking with heart creates a non-threatening workplace where people are free to share their opinions and views respectfully. Voice impacts how people respond to situations and influences the heart of others—good or bad. Being aware of your voice when communicating with your team is a priority to assure your message is heard and understood. Those who lead with heart in voice:

- Dialogue with heart
- Talk with instead of talk at
- Choose words carefully, strategically
- Carry the message with clarity, firmness, and respect
- Understand defensiveness

- Laughter is the best medicine
- Delivery
- Body talk
- Tone
- Writing etiquette

Dialogue with heart

Words mean more than what is set down on paper. It takes the human voice to infuse them with deeper meaning. ~Maya Angelou

Real dialogue can often lead to understanding, helping communities to get along much better. ~Robert Alan

Two monologues do not make a dialogue. ~Jeff Daly

The most important thing in communication is to hear what isn't being said.
~Peter F. Drucker

Dialogues take place under a variety of circumstances. They are a two-way conversation that is only possible when one party speaks, the other listens, and then the roles are reversed. Dialoging with heart means to speak and listen to others with an attitude of interest, empathy, compassion, and respect. The ability to speak with people respectfully and honorably is an empowering tool in leadership and life.

Being able to converse with others using the heart as your guide is a gift that should be practiced no matter your level in the organization. Dialoguing with heart shows people you care about them. It includes asking questions to elicit thoughtful reflection. People respond positively to a calm and understanding voice. Speaking from the heart soothes the soul. It can inspire, direct, and potentially move people from an emotional state to a rational state in times of stress.

Voice is about self-expression and allows you to affirm your beliefs. When having conversations, speak from your own heart, not the heart of others. Conversations driven by the heart will enhance communication and open doors to successful partnerships and innovation.

Gentle Reminder:

A leader's voice can inspire action.

Reflections:

- How have you used your voice to influence a situation?

- What are some "voices" that you use?

- Do you ever consciously modulate your voice to make a point?

- What are some tactics for turning a monologue into a dialogue?

- Have you had to calm down an employee or client recently?

- What strategy did you use to redirect?

- When communicating with this person or your team do you consistently use your own beliefs and passions to drive the conversation?

- Is most of your day spent telling people what to do or is it spent discovering what is being done through conversation?

Talking with instead of talking at

Being a role model for thinking, planning, and problem solving feeds the synergy you are trying to create throughout your organization. All staff meetings, coaching, training, and professional development must be presented (delivered) and structured in a way that reflects what is expected in the work place. If you model a "stand and deliver" or "talking to/at" delivery style as part of your facilitating strategy then you are giving your team permission to do the same to those they lead. Talking at your team without engaging them in the thinking and planning gives the impression that you know everything (close minded). This approach can block creativity and initiative.

When you talk with your team, you are modeling your expectations of a process grounded in inclusion rather than exclusion. Talking with your team encourages collective critical and analytical thinking, facilitated, not dictated, by you. Redirect questions, concerns, and issues back to the team by modeling your thinking and guiding them to solutions. Encourage communication to be conversations, not dictations or monologues.

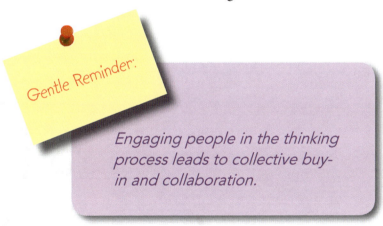

Gentle Reminder:

Engaging people in the thinking process leads to collective buy-in and collaboration.

Voice

Reflections:

- When facilitating meetings and conferences, do you answer all questions asked or do you redirect the questions back to the team to solve collectively?

- Consider your own communication style—who does most of the talking when you are meeting with the people you lead?

Choose words carefully, strategically

Words create conceptions and self-conceptions.... Choosing words carefully is a moral responsibility. ~Amos Oz

The difference between the right word and the almost right word is the difference between lightning and a lightning bug. ~Mark Twain.

I waited and waited, and when no message came, I knew it must have been from you. ~Ashleigh Brilliant

Your choice of words is part of building a professional culture and respectful relationship amongst team members. Being calm, careful, and strategic when choosing your words will earn you respect and will give people something to think about. We must choose our words carefully and strategically for the type of communication in which we are engaged. For example, the words you use to report status to management might be significantly different from those you use to instruct a new team member, or when making a presentation to your peers. Your words and how you deliver them have the potential to inspire or demotivate; to impact behavioral changes or bring about desired actions.

Think before you speak. No one will mind if you take a deep breath before responding to a question or if you ask for a moment to reflect and collect your thoughts before you answer.

In stressful situations (for example, confrontation, an angry team member, bad news, etc.), my father always said count to ten before you respond so you don't lose your cool. When someone comes to you with a complaint, keep the problem or issue in the lap of the one who brought it by removing emotion from your response. Stay calm and plan your words carefully—your calmness can sometimes fuel another person's emotion or diminish it.

When confronted or when someone speaks to you in an unprofessional manner, stay focused on what is truly happening and remember they have made the choice of how to speak to you. When these people don't succeed at getting you rattled or angry, they may try again—be prepared and remember integrity and heart.

"Don't let the turkeys get you down" is a popular saying for a reason. Stay focused on what the person is really saying; use their words and phrases in your response (taking notes during the interaction helps). Avoid put-downs and stay away from I...I...I...when responding. Its not about you, so keep the "I" out of it. Ask for clarification when something offensive is said; write down the person's words so you can respond based on their actual concerns. If you are not ready to respond on the spot, then reschedule the discussion, giving yourself time to reflect.

When coaching, counseling, presenting, or facilitating conversations, be careful how you phrase potentially controversial points. Practice ahead of time if it's something that can be planned.

Be sure your message is clear, and be mindful of what you say, as your words may be repeated or misquoted by others.

Gentle Reminder:

> Choice of words affects how relationships are built. Words can hurt and cause animosity and distrust. Count to ten before responding to a situation that ruffles your feathers.

Reflections:
- What are your favorite words of encouragement?

- What words do you use to describe success?

- What words would you avoid in handling conflict?

- Have your words ever been quoted back to you? How did they sound?

- Can you think of a time when someone was confrontational (disrespectful) with you...what was the situation? How did you respond? Any regrets? If you had to do it over again—what changes would you make? What did you learn from the experience?

Carry the message with clarity, firmness, and respect

Whenever you have truth it must be given with love, or the message and the messenger will be rejected. ~Mahatma Gandhi

When we have the courage to speak out—to break our silence—we inspire the rest of the "moderates" in our communities to speak up and voice their views. ~Sharon Schuster

The way we communicate with others and with ourselves ultimately determines the quality of our lives. ~Anthony Robbins

Your leadership voice needs to be clear and firm to reflect the true meaning of your message. Articulate your message with heart by using a positive yet resolved approach. Articulate for clarity, effectiveness, and empowerment. Avoid using filler words like um, ah, …. Using filler words gives the impression you are not totally confident or comfortable with the message you are delivering.

Use your core beliefs about building relationships and avoid threats and fear-driven messaging—a practice used by power-driven leaders.

Demonstrate respect by avoiding put-downs and words that could be condescending or rude. Keep your messages succinct and to the point to avoid misunderstandings and misinterpretations.

Gentle Reminder:

Short messages have greater power than long ones.

Reflections:
- What does it mean to be articulate?

- Do you find yourself using filler words when speaking?

- Is it difficult for you to speak in public?

- How hard is it for you to give a negative message?

- When you are misunderstood, how do you rectify the miscommunication?

Understand defensiveness

One of the greatest gifts of leadership is to recognize your own defensive behavior, acknowledge it, learn from it, and move on. ~Laurie Hinzman

The only person who is educated is the one who has learned how to learn—and change. ~Carl Rogers

If you start a conversation with the assumption that you are right or that you must win, obviously it is difficult to talk. ~Wendell Berry

Those who take pride in their work may get their feathers ruffled when they find themselves defending their decisions and/or actions. The toughest line of defense is when someone has judged another unfairly and/or used a disrespectful tone or inflection in their voice when communicating. Leaders, while often the receivers of criticism, are also responsible for critiquing the work of others…keep criticism constructive and positive. Most people are sensitive to the potential threat of criticism as it can attack the recipient's confidence or ego (self-image). The defensive response is natural but can cause a situation to escalate to a point where one is viewed as being insubordinate or uncooperative.

Defending one's work does not have to evolve into a confrontation. When being confronted with criticism, keep the heart work in the forefront of response. Stand tall and listen to what is being said. If you recognize your own defensiveness, acknowledge it, step away from the situation and reflect on your actions and reactions. Have the courage to respond in a way that doesn't feed the criticism negatively but shows flexibility in accepting feedback. Avoid showing your defensiveness on your face or through your body language. Practice taking criticism with dignity, say "thank you for sharing", learn from it (because the criticism might be warranted), and develop a follow up plan that addresses the critique. Avoid subtle put-downs in the midst of your frustration or stress caused by criticism. Recognize that sometimes others are right and you are wrong. Understand that when you are critiquing the work of others they will have the same feelings about being critiqued.

To avoid defensiveness when critiquing, use words of praise and support to open your conversation—point out the positives first, then include the team member in discovering the areas of need. Ask questions that give them an opportunity to explain the thinking behind the work being discussed. Facilitate feedback to the point where your critique becomes an integrated process in the debriefing, then offer suggestions and next steps through coaching and support.

Gentle Reminder:

Defensive communication (voice) and behavior can lead to resistance, which negatively impacts the achievement of goals.

Reflections:

- When do you find yourself being defensive?

- Is it possible for simply the tone of voice to provoke defensiveness in the person you're speaking to?

- How do you handle someone who has attacked your character or work?

- Can you think of a time when you have been defensive? What was the circumstance? If you had to do it over again, what would you do differently?

- Can you think of a time when you provoked defensive behavior in someone?

- How do you respond to critiques?

- Have you ever had to admit you made a mistake? How did it feel? What was the circumstance? What lesson did you learn from the experience?

Laughter is the best medicine

I am thankful for laughter, except when milk comes out of my nose.
~Woody Allen

At the height of laughter, the universe is flung into a kaleidoscope of new possibilities. ~Jean Houston

Laughter creates a positive emotional climate and a sense of connection between people. People are brought together through laughter. It improves job performance because it is a natural stress reducer. It can diffuse tense situations and make good times even better. There is also evidence that laughter increases blood flow rich in oxygen to support heart and brain health. Laughter along with a sense of humor is heart healthy and needs to be embedded in verbal and written communication. It's comforting, healing, and good for the soul. Remember to laugh at yourself and laugh with others.

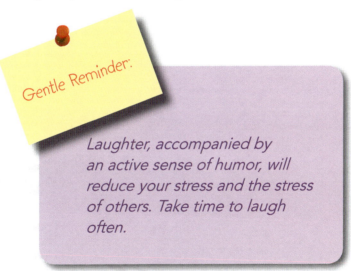

Gentle Reminder:

Laughter, accompanied by an active sense of humor, will reduce your stress and the stress of others. Take time to laugh often.

Reflections:
- Did you laugh today?

- Do you make time to engage in laughter with your team?

- How do you incorporate humor into your verbal and written communications?

- Do you observe laughter amongst your team members?

Delivery

It is delivery that makes the orator's success. ~Johann Wolfgang von Goethe

You can speak well if your tongue can deliver the message of your heart.
~John Ford

In addition to your choice of words, voice inflections and body movements help create a delivery style that is an important part of effective and meaningful communication. Think about how you use eye contact and body language to promote buy-in. Delivery from the heart means that through your knowledge and expertise you are able to convey messages in a way that directly connects to the work of those you lead. Messages delivered from the heart will be more powerful, inspirational, and meaningful towards the success and achievement of results in your organization.

A strong leadership voice will be heard with heart if it is delivered from the heart. The impact your delivery style has during meetings, trainings, and conferences determines whether the audience fully engages and leaves motivated, energized, and prepared to take their new learning into their practice. During my professional career, I have experienced various styles of delivery from "experts" who have either captured me as a learner or had me wondering why I was there. One of the most non-engaging and unimpressive delivery styles is when leaders read from their notes or read a PowerPoint— word for word. They were not just reading from their notes for a short time but throughout the whole session with little to no eye contact or audience participation. I've also had to sit through sessions where presenters use what I call "textbook language", the voice of others, for the whole presentation.

When you're sitting in a presentation and someone is reading to you it's a waste of your time—nothing is being added to the message—so why should you listen to someone reading their PowerPoint presentation when they could have sent it to you and you could simply read it yourself.

When giving a presentation, use your heart, not your notes. While recognizing notes and outlines of a message are needed and serve a purpose in the organization of thought, the message is more powerful and empowering when it is delivered from the heart of the presenter based on a very real belief and knowledge base. Leaders have a greater opportunity to inspire and influence productivity when they use their own voice and expertise when sharing ideas, suggestions, and solutions. Reading a research paper or pre-written notes word for word or speaking textbook language reduces leadership credibility. If you cannot present the information without reading notes word for word, then find someone else who is knowledgeable about the content area to do the presentation.

When speaking to an audience, effective leaders engage in the constant practice of "audience watch". The participation (buy-in) of the audience you are presenting to, regardless of the setting, matters. Keep a watchful eye on their body language and attitude. Make it a practice to read facial expressions, listen to voice intonations when responding to questions, and check for eye contact (attention). Are they sitting up straight in their chairs? Are they taking notes? Are they responsive to your inquiries? Are they nodding off or, heaven forbid, sleeping? It's your responsibility as a leader to ensure your delivery is engaging and keeps active listening and participation a priority. If your audience watch tells you that they are not engaged, it is your job to adapt your presentation. There is nothing wrong with changing plans in mid-stream—reflection throughout the delivery is key to ensure you are connecting with your audience. If you as the leader cannot capture the full attention of the audience, then it's you who needs to change.

Your leadership voice through delivery serves as a model for others and needs to be treated as such. If it isn't working then change it until it is. The greatest opportunity to connect with your team is made during conferences, trainings, staff meetings, and individual conversations. Speak from experience, engage with heart, watch your audience, and use notes as a guide only.

Effective and meaningful delivery also includes the ability to capture multiple learning styles throughout the presentation. When presenting, ask yourself... is my delivery auditory only (linguistic learners) or do I have visuals to accompany my presentation? Are my PowerPoints, handouts, etc. in black and white or have I added color to capture the visual learners in the group? Understanding the research on Multiple Intelligences (Howard Gardner) will assist any leader in organizing, planning and facilitating presentations that meet the needs of all participants. In any company, business, political, or educational setting, acknowledging and respecting the fact that not all people acquire knowledge in the same way is to honor and respect individual talent and expertise. Incorporating this research and knowledge into your delivery will provide equal and fair access to information being presented.

Gentle Reminder:

Knowing how each of your team members acquires new knowledge is the key to opening doors for promoting continuous growth. Knowing and presenting to the learning styles of your team provides equal access to new learning which encourages all to stay engaged.

Reflections:

- What learning style(s) do you have?

- What is your dominant learning style?

- Do you recognize the learning style of those you lead? List all known.

- What steps can you take to learn what learning styles exist within your organization?

- Do you talk about what you expect or do you show it?

- When you present or facilitate a meeting do you use visuals? Are they in color?

- How do you ensure your team is continuously learning?

- When you present, how do you provide opportunities for audience participation?

Body talk

In the delivery process, a large percentage of non-verbal communication is derived through body language which I refer to as body talk. Body talk can influence how people interpret conversations, discussions, and messages. It is an important part of the communication process and is driven by a person's emotions, attitude, or current state of mind. A heartfelt communication voice includes an understanding of how one can and cannot use their body to say what they mean. Facial expressions, eye movement, crossing of arms, stance, sighs, etc. all play a role in the interpretations (or misinterpretations) of any message being delivered or received.

Stay aware of your body language, no matter how you feel. Keep the heart in it and never let them see you sweat during confrontational or uncomfortable situations. Be aware that impressions matter and make sure your body talk sends the message you want to project. Maintain an air of confidence and professionalism and avoid giving others a chance to misinterpret based on unintentional or subconscious gestures and facial expressions.

Gentle Reminder:

Get to know your own body talk and practice not wearing your emotions on your sleeve.

Reflections:
- Do you use your hands when you are talking?

- Are you animated while you are talking?

- Can you think of a time when your body talk gave a wrong impression? What happened?

- How big of an impact do you feel facial expressions have in communication?

- Do you have an expression that you do all the time—your signature expression?

- Do you feel you wear your emotions on your sleeve? If yes, in what way? Do others?

Tone

Don't look at me in that tone of voice! ~David Farber

When he has a meeting, he doesn't have to scream and yell, he can just give you that face and that tone he has, and you know we had better pick it up and get going again. ~Tino Martinez

Watch your tone with me, young lady! ~Mom

We often refuse to accept an idea merely because the tone of voice in which it has been expressed is unsympathetic to us. ~Friedrich Nietzsche

Tone of voice reflects your attitude and state of mind in the moment. The way you say something frames the message and influences its intent. Tone is echoed (delivered) through voice intonations and is a direct result of education, morals, upbringing, mood, manners, and philosophical outlook on life. The tone you use can signify strength, confidence, understanding, compassion, arrogance, anger, envy, interest, condescension, and a multitude of other characteristics. Pay attention to your tone and how you respond to the tone of others.

Awareness is the first step toward ensuring tone does not interfere with your leadership voice and the message you are delivering.

Gentle Reminder:

It's the way you say it that people tend to focus on, not the content.

Voice

Reflections:

- Does anyone on your team carry a "rude" tone? Are they angry? Is it just their nature?

- When someone speaks to you in a certain tone, do you match their tone in your response? Is that a good idea?

Writing etiquette

There's nothing to writing. All you do is sit down at a computer and open a vein. ~Walter Wellesley "Red" Smith

The wastebasket is a writer's best friend. ~Isaac Bashevis Singer

Words are just words and without heart they have no meaning.
~Chinese Proverb

Writing is a powerful way to express leadership voice. The written word can address visions and goals, celebrate excellence and successes, promote synergy, honor experts, provide updates, and cheer people on. It can serve as a gentle reminder of expectations and timelines. The written word is also used to express concern for poor job performance and/or service. Whatever the need for the writing, a leader with heart will ensure that the voice expressed in the writing is clear, grounded in core beliefs, succinct, and based on facts. Writing remains long after words have been spoken. When writing promotional or inspirational material...passion, hopes, dreams, goals can drive the words. However, if the writing addresses job performance (personnel or results) then facts, not emotion, must drive the words. Be reflective with your writing, choose words carefully, use spell check...play the devil's advocate to ensure nothing has been written that isn't true—that you say what you mean and mean what you say. Once something is in writing it becomes a paper trail. Some people need to express their frustrations in writing to make themselves feel better. There's nothing wrong with "venting" using the written word as long as you don't share it with others. Before sending your writing, set it down, give it a rest, then return to it later and reread to be sure your message is clear, concise, consistent, and complete. You may even want to ask a trusted associate to review it for you before sending.

Emails and text messages are in the public domain and can be accessed if needed, even after you think you have deleted them. Don't send anything in an email or text message that could possibly come back to haunt you. Remember, once you press the "Send" button, your words cannot be retracted. Stay focused on the purpose of your writing and make sure your true voice (leadership, heart) is represented. Write with the big picture in mind.

Gentle Reminder:
Never put in writing something that could come back to haunt you.

Reflections:

- How do you assure your writing is clear, concise?

- What do your words say about you?

- In what ways do you consider your audience when writing?

- Have you ever put in writing something you regretted?

- Have you ever had to justify something you have written?

- Have you ever received something in writing that ruffled your feathers? How did you handle it? What steps, if any, did you take to address it?

- Do you feel you're a good writer?

- Do you enjoy writing?

- Are you good with grammar and spelling? Do you consistently use spell check?

- Do you use writing to promote greatness within your organization?

- What type (genre) of writing is your strongest? Weakest?

- Do you proofread your writing?

> Walk the talk and dance the dance—
> it is contagious and makes a difference.
> ~Laurie Hinzman

model

> Role models set goals for you and try to make you as good as they are. Role models are important. ~Kasey Zacharias

> To know how to suggest is the great art of teaching. ~Henri Frederic Amiel

> If your actions inspire others to dream more, learn more, do more and become more, you are a leader.
> ~John Quincy Adams

Modeling is demonstrating steps needed to accomplish the vision and goals of the organization. Modeling is part of leadership's heart work because your passion and commitment to the work are exemplified by the daily expression of your beliefs, expectations, decisions, and follow-through. Excellent performance and the striving for personal best are essential elements in achieving success and greatness. When you expect it from yourself, it will be obvious and become contagious. A leader with heart models passion and dedication to the profession. The essential components to modeling, which should be an expectation, not an exception, include:

- Practice what you preach—walk the talk
- Own your behavior
- Learn from mistakes
- Solution vs. problem
- Project a professional image
- First impressions, manners, and etiquette

Practice what you preach...walk the talk

If you think practicing what you preach is rough, just try preaching what you practice. ~Bowen Baxter

An ounce of practice is worth a pound of preaching. ~Proverb

Action is eloquence. ~William Shakespeare

The values and beliefs you share with people need to be obvious every moment of your work day. Part of building relationships and trust in the organization is the ability to be a role model in all aspects of the work—the ability to model gives you credibility and respect as the leader of the work. What you expect from others needs to be expected of yourself and modeled by you. Modeling is part of a unified approach in achieving desired outcomes and needs to be congruent, real, and heart-connected. Walking the talk, not just talking the talk, exemplifies a "we are all in this together" work attitude and positively impacts productivity. Expectations must be modeled, connected, and flow between leaders and colleagues to ensure the work is integrated, not fragmented. The ability to model your core beliefs, expertise, understanding of the work, integrity, problem solving strategies, and standards of behavior gives you credibility. It shows people you are among the experts in the field and that you understand the complexity and details of the work that needs to be accomplished at all levels.

The expectations you carry for yourself serve as a guide and model for those to follow. If a leader expects people to work together collaboratively and respectfully then the leader must do the same. They should unconditionally be incorporated into the walk and talk of the daily routine. If you expect personal best, then you must give it as well. If a leader expects people to coach one another, then the leader must use coaching in their practice as well. If a coach expects good sportsmanship, then they must model it themselves. If a leader expects heart then they must use heart. There must be an attitude of what's good for me is good for you—actions cannot send a message that exemplify double standards. You do it...they in turn will do it with one another and with you. Walk the talk, it's contagious and must be the rule, not the exception.

Being present and visible throughout the organization exemplifies the fact you are part of the team and that you care. Be present at collaboratives and planning sessions. Meet and greet people every day with direct eye contact, salutation, and supporting smile. Make a point of acknowledging all members of the organization regardless of their level.

Gentle Reminder:

Your attitude makes a difference and is contagious—wear it on your sleeve with pride.

Reflections:

- How do you model your core beliefs?

- How do you model the vision and goals of the organization?

- How do you actively engage yourself in the work?

- How does upper management in your organization model their expectations?

- Do you make it a point to say good morning to all you see?

- Do you make eye contact with a smile with people who pass by?

Own your behavior

Behavior is the mirror in which everyone shows their image. ~Goethe

You are the only one who gives permission for your actions. You are the only one who gives permission for you to act the way you act. ~Laurie Hinzman

Your behavior—what you do and how you do it, is at the core of modeling and leadership. No one controls your behavior except you—you **own** it. Behavior is the result of education, training, morals, and character. It can, of course, be affected by factors such as stress, health issues, and other challenges. Your attitude is contagious and makes a difference.

Excellence and the striving for personal best are essential elements in achieving success and greatness. If you expect it from yourself it will be obvious. These essentials fuel the work and must be an expectation not an exception.

A leader with heart will own (accept responsibility for) their own behavior and choices. Owning our behavior means being honest with ourselves and others, admitting mistakes, and rectifying them. It is a sign of a mature individual. We all have personal and professional stress factors which influence or impact our behaviors and challenge our heart, integrity, and character. If we "wake up on the wrong side of the bed" tired or frustrated, we may say things that are out of character or we might react negatively to a situation without warrant. It's our professional obligation to accept responsibility for our actions regardless of what side of the bed we woke up on.

People who lead with the heart take time to reflect on their behaviors during the day. However, sometimes things don't go as planned and you may be faced with the reality that you are not perfect. Sometimes you will err in judgment, action, or opinions, and things won't go the way you thought they would. Reflecting helps us understand the "why" and the "how" of our behavior. With renewed understanding, it can put us back on the right path.

Model

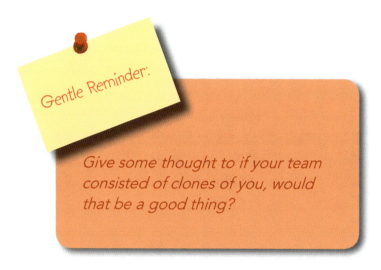

Gentle Reminder:

Give some thought to if your team consisted of clones of you, would that be a good thing?

Reflections:

- Try keeping a reflections journal tracking your behavior. What was the highlight of the day? When were you proudest of what you did? Is there something you did today that you'd like to do over?

- How does stress affect your behavior?

- What are some constructive uses of stress?

Learn from mistakes

Some mistakes are too much fun to only make once. ~Brad Paisley

Mistakes are acts of learning. ~Laurie Hinzman

Mistakes are sometimes the best memories. ~Lake Fimspin

You're born, you die, and in between you make a lot of mistakes.
~Anonymous

Sometimes inadequate knowledge or inaccurate information has led us to make a poor decision, sometimes it's due to a misunderstanding or misconception. The fact is—mistakes happen and are part of life. It's human nature to make mistakes, they happen to everyone. Acknowledging this, it is important to incorporate your heart into dealing with mistakes; they need to be addressed regardless of who makes them.

Mistakes come with being human; however, with mistakes comes opportunity. They should be viewed as an opportunity for learning and used as stepping stones toward personal and professional growth as long as they are not repeated over and over again. It's our responsibility as leaders to seize the opportunity offered by a mistake and do something productive with it. A leader who leads with the heart will admit when mistakes are made and will also model steps taken to rectify them. A leader who is transparent about their own mistakes and steps they took to fix them conveys their own fallibility and commitment to life-long growth and learning. Turn mistakes into learning by reflecting on why they happened, revisiting what went wrong, committing to never repeating them, and turning your new learning into something even stronger. Model this belief with your team and expect them to become proactive in their experiences with mistakes.

Be dedicated to lifelong learning, learn from mistakes and successes, and build each day upon the work from yesterday. We only get better at our craft if we learn as we go…enduring and facing the bumps and bruises with an understanding heart and when necessary, a big dose of forgiveness. When

Model

mistakes are identified, use them as an opportunity to coach towards next steps. No one is perfect and to expect perfection is unrealistic. If you expect your organization to be progressive, then mistakes will be made because progressiveness takes people out of their comfort zone and hopefully into new learning that will serve to benefit the greater good.

Gentle Reminder:

If you don't learn from your mistakes, you'll keep repeating them until you do.

Reflections:

- What is your definition of "mistake"?

- Do you make mistakes?

- Is it easy for you to admit you have made a mistake?

- If it's hard for you to admit your fallibility, explain why.

- What is one of the most recent work-related mistakes you made? How did you handle it?

- What is a recent mistake that has happened among your team? How did you facilitate the learning from it? What was the outcome? What steps were taken to rectify the situation?

Solution vs. problem

Leaders are problem solvers by talent and temperament, and by choice.
~Harlan Cleveland

Most people spend more time and energy going around problems than in trying to solve them. ~Henry Ford

Hot heads and cold hearts never solved anything. ~Billy Graham

When the only tool you own is a hammer, every problem begins to resemble a nail. ~Abraham Maslow

Leaders need to keep their minds focused on the vision and goals of the business and not be inundated with the "problems" inherent with all occupations. Encouraging the heart when it comes to facing issues and concerns means to expect people to be part of the solution or it is assumed they are part of the problem. No one has time to be bogged down with problems, complaints, and minutia. If people have time to voice complaints then they also have time to think of possible solutions. It's imperative for a leader to model and set a precedent that when complaints, issues, or concerns are shared, it is expected that possible solutions need to be shared as well. We are all in this together; therefore, together we can make changes for the better. Encouraging all team members to be proactive with issues and answers adds to the synergy of the organization. Engaging multiple brains in problem solving is powerful stuff.

When you have heart-to-heart talks with your team, model the thinking that goes into launching possible solutions to problems by engaging the team in the fact-finding mission that leads to possible solutions. For every problem, there are many possible solutions; therefore, for every problem shared, the one sharing needs to be prepared to offer viable solutions that enable the work to continue. When asked for clarification to a problem—redirect/reframe the question by asking what they think the problem is. Guide them to discover the answer themselves. This is time consuming; however, the more you do it, the more it becomes innate. Guide people by showing you understand what they are going through—help them find solutions so they can redirect their attention to the work. It's up to the leader to decide if the solution is fair and benefits the greater good. Collective problem solving leads to faster solutions which promote efficiency and productivity.

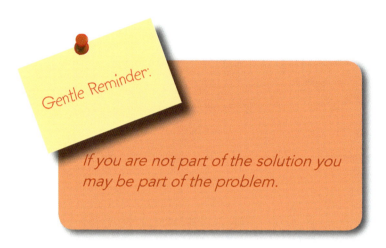

Gentle Reminder:

If you are not part of the solution you may be part of the problem.

Reflections:
- What policies do you have to encourage people to be active problem solvers?

- Do you solve all work-related problems unilaterally or do you encourage people to seek and propose solutions before they come to you?

- What is your policy on people sharing complaints?

- How do you communicate solutions to problems?

Project a professional image

Professional image is about setting standards of excellence, starting with your attire and behavior and extending to the physical environment you create in your workspace. Professional image that comes from the heart is also modeled by the way people treat one another, regardless of whether they are part of the team or stakeholders such as clients or visitors. Image should reflect the expectations you have for yourself and those who work with you. Professional attire serves as a model for an image that commands respect. It is well known in all walks of life that people are treated based on their appearance regardless of who they are and what they know.

Your choice of clothing and personal grooming will set the stage for how seriously people take you. If you dress casually, that is how people will view you in the workplace. If you dress professionally, the same is true. Command respect by presenting yourself in a professional manner and expect the same from the people you work with. People will talk and behave professionally when they are around others who dress the part. Modeling professionalism is what separates you and your team from amateurs.

The appearance and condition of the work environment also portrays the image of the organization. It's the responsibility of the leader to ensure the appearance of the workplace exemplifies its standards, expectations, visions, and goals. A few ideas of how to encourage the heart through an environment that demonstrates pride are:

- A clutter-free environment inside and out is pleasing to the eye and reflects a sense of order and pride
- Color schemes (warm tones) on walls are important and can be used to create a warm and inviting atmosphere
- Furniture should be comfortable and conducive to the work being performed
- Round tables placed in meeting and conference rooms promote collaboration
- Ensure the landscaping is healthy, trimmed, and free of weeds
- Colorful flowering plants in the landscaping add beauty and class

Model

Gentle Reminder:

We cannot change the way people view us upon our first meeting; however, we do have the choice to make sure they are impressed by the way we present ourselves and our organization inside and out.

Model

Reflections:

- What do you wear to work every day? Why?

- Does your attire set precedence for others to follow?

- How would you describe the way you dress?

- Is there a dress code within your organization for all levels?

- Do you expect people to dress professionally? What is professional dress?

- Is your work environment neat and organized?

- How does your work environment exemplify your organization's visions and goals?

- Where do you have meetings and how do you have the tables and chairs arranged?

- What are the color schemes inside and out of your offices?

- In their workplaces, do people sit facing the door or with their backs to the door?

- How do your offices reflect expectations?

Model

First impressions, manners, and etiquette

Etiquette is behaving yourself a little better than is absolutely necessary.
~Will Cuppy

Image matters, especially when it comes to first impressions. Manners, etiquette, and first impressions are worth mentioning because they have such an impact on how people perceive you. It's human nature to formulate opinions based on actions and first impressions. A person can tell another person's state of mind and approach to life during a first encounter.

There is no doubt that first impressions do make a lasting impression on others. They evolve from your mannerisms, attitude, appearance, and environment. First impressions, which include the written word, can either get you a job or not, open a door or not, encourage collaboration or not, gain respect or not… you get the picture. First impressions matter and should be taken seriously.

Good manners and following the accepted rules of business etiquette are important aspects of social behavior and must be modeled by all team members. When the leader models and expects people to practice good manners and professionalism, it becomes an unconditional standard throughout the company.

As a leader, you should expect common courtesy, manners, and an awareness of other people's feelings to be integrated throughout the day, every day. An empowering environment is one that promotes kindness, sensitivity, and consideration for others. Some people have a natural instinct to be courteous while others need gentle reminders. There should be no negotiation or compromise on how we act around others—none.

Model

Gentle Reminder:

Give some thought to what people think the first time they meet you; the first time they walk into your organization. It's worth your time.

Model

Reflections:

- What are your expectations of the appearance of your work environment?

- How does your work environment exemplify your expectations of yourself and employees?

- Is the environment warm and inviting? In what ways?

- Is your work place free from clutter? How do you handle the clutter of others?

- How does your office staff greet people in person and on the phone?

- Do your employees practice good manners? How do you know?

- Are the team members cordial with one another and with you?

- Do people greet others with a smile—do people say good morning to one another?

- Do you say please, thank you, and I'm sorry? Do you expect the same from those you work with?

guide

> A leader who coaches to inspire, motivate, energize, and elicit intellectual excitement in those they lead is a leader who leads with passion and heart.
> *-Laurie Hinzman*

> The world of the 1990s and beyond will not belong to managers or those who can make numbers dance. The world will belong to the passionate, driven leaders—people who not only have enormous amounts of energy but who can energize those whom they lead.
> *-Jack Welch*

Guiding plays an important role in the heart work because it is what keeps the heart in the work. Using the heart to guide people towards achieving results creates a work environment that is synergized and energized in personal best because it is based on trust, not threat. Guiding is about encouraging employees to think creatively, work collaboratively, and keep passion as a driving force for their work. The practice of guiding serves as an avenue for continuous learning and invokes deeper thinking from the people in the organization. It is crucial that people understand you are a leader who facilitates thinking, not one who dictates thinking.

The role of an effective leader is to facilitate and coach based on identified needs. Guiding is not about a dictatorship—it is about facilitating thinking that impacts the ability for all the people to grow. It's a practice that empowers people to want to learn and continue building their competence and abilities knowing they will be appreciated and respected as long as their efforts support the vision and goals of the organization. Guiding with the intent to increase knowledge levels and expertise should be a goal practiced and implemented by all leaders who expect results. Engaging team members in meaningful dialogue that focuses on individual skill sets builds upon strengths and reduces weaknesses. Work to build confidence in people by honestly speaking from your heart.

Guiding is also about letting go and gradually releasing responsibility and trust to your team members. It's an act of giving people the freedom to use their skills and expertise for the betterment of the organization, in efforts to increase production, improve relations with clients, and raise achievement.

Guiding is appropriate for the majority of situations, but there are also times when a very direct approach needs to be taken, for example, in the case of insubordination or a failure to follow instructions.

Guiding is the use of inquiry (questioning)—getting people to understand, in depth, the steps that support the work they are doing.

Good listening skills are also essential to assist team members with self-discovery while supporting the big picture or plan—the organization's vision.

Guiding is embedded in the acts of coaching and mentoring. Being able to be a mentor and a coach to those you lead will enable people to be proactive in their thinking process and offer a new perspective to the work being done. Effective leaders recognize the importance of providing opportunities that encourage continuous growth. Working with your team gives them a chance to be reflective, with your guidance, in their day-to-day practice.

Effective guiding practices include:

- Heart-to-heart
- Guide according to the big picture
- Coach with greatness and success in mind
- Keep expectations high and realistic
- Sage on the stage vs. guide on the side
- Emotion vs. passion and professionalism
- Listen with a full heart, watch, and take notes
- Feedback—firm, inquisitive, thought-provoking
- Redirect with suggestions, accountability, and timelines
- Reflection
- Reflection vs. reaction

Heart-to-heart

My guiding principles in life are to be honest, genuine, thoughtful and caring.
~Prince William

Speaking from your heart allows the emotionally difficult, the ordinary, and the wonderful things in our lives to be communicated and received.
~David McArthur and Bruce McArthur

Without credible communication, and a lot of it, employee hearts and minds are never captured. ~John P. Kotter

Heart-to-heart is about articulating the vision, which is the future, in a non-threatening, honest, and passionate way. It is about addressing realities and building relationships based on truth and trust. Trust and honesty with those who work with you guides the coaching and mentoring process. A heart-to-heart leadership style also gives team members an opportunity to be open and honest, respectfully, about their accomplishments, challenges, and failures. People have unlimited potential. During whole group, small group, or individual meetings, make it a habit to have "heart to hearts" with your team. Heart-driven messaging has the potential to elicit "performance with pride" in the workplace.

Gentle Reminder:

When we believe in and nurture the hearts of all team members, we create an energy-filled environment.

Reflections:

- How can you tell when people are honest with you when they are sharing their thoughts and opinions?

- When you address your team do you feel you speak from the heart?

- What does "heart-to-heart" mean to you?

Guide according to the big picture

Vision without action is merely a dream. Action without vision just passes the time. Vision with action can change the world. ~Joel Barker

The shepherd always tries to persuade the sheep that their interests and his own are the same. ~Henri B. Stendhal

Leaders establish the vision for the future and set the strategy for getting there; they cause change. They motivate and inspire others to go in the right direction and they, along with everyone else, sacrifice to get there.

~John Kotter

A good coach passes on information quickly. They do not hold back information that affects my job. ~Byron & Catherine Pulsifer

An effective leader guides with the big picture in mind and sees things that others do not see. The big picture represents the purpose, direction, goals, and expected outcomes of the organization. It is the organization's vision about the future and requires mutual commitment and dedication to achieve.

Guiding according to the big picture is about applying lessons from the past with the future in mind. Offering support and guidance incorporates the identification, analysis, and understanding of "the big picture". Guiding with the big picture in mind means that decisions are not made in isolation or to support personal/political agendas, but are made for the good of the entire organization. Your guiding words need to inspire, motivate, and encourage activities in support of the organization's core beliefs, vision, and goals.

Gentle Reminder:

Attaining and staying focused on the "big picture" takes a lot of dedicated effort and can't be achieved without buy-in from everyone on the team.

Reflections:

- Describe what the "big picture" is for your organization.

- How does the big picture correlate to your organization's vision and goal statements?

- If you asked three people in your organization, how would they define the big picture?

- What steps have you taken to ensure everyone understands what the big picture is?

Coach with greatness and success in mind

True leadership lies in guiding others to success. It is ensuring that everyone is performing at their best, doing the work they are pledged to do and doing it well. ~Bill Owens

Probably my best quality as a coach is that I ask a lot of challenging questions and let the person come up with the answer. ~Phil Dixon

Treat a man as he is, he will remain so. Treat a man the way he can be and ought to be, and he will become as he can be and should be.
~Johann Wolfgang von Goethe

To coach with greatness and success in mind, the leader must know who their team members are, their strengths, and weaknesses. They must be able to encourage, support, and guide team members in their pursuits. Coaching with greatness comes from passion, not from the job title you currently hold. Use your own passion to inspire and motivate your team to do their personal best towards achieving success. Coaching is an opportunity to nurture passion in others while staying focused on achieving desired results.

Coaching effectively comes from the ability to draw from your own experiences. Hopefully you have been promoted to your position based on your experiences, expertise, and accomplishments. It's important to draw on those so you can coach with understanding and success.

Coaching is about taking people to the next step or the next level; it is building on their strengths and providing new possibilities to expand and improve performance. When people feel encouraged and supported, they are inspired to become better at their craft. When coaching becomes common practice (part of the norm instead of the exception) and entrenched in the day-to-day work, it becomes contagious...people feel empowered to guide one another instead of work in isolation.

A leader with heart knows who the key players are...nurture them. The hope for any successful organization is that the movers and shakers (catalysts, achievers) will outnumber those who wish to remain at the status quo. Coaching from the heart empowers the movers and shakers to influence the commitment, work, and results of everyone else to the point where those who lounge in the status quo have no choice but to either join in or leave.

Gentle Reminder:

Coaching with greatness is creating the energy that encourages people to think out of the box and develop new skills that will lead to successful outcomes.

Reflections:

- In what ways do you consider yourself to be a coach?

- How does coaching at work resemble coaching a sports team?

- What are some of the strengths and weaknesses of the people you lead?

- Create a chart that lists your strengths and weaknesses and those of your team members.

- List your "movers and shakers" (leaders)...your followers...and those who wish to stay status quo.

- Do you mentor a leadership team?

- If so who are they? If not—who would you choose?

- How do you lead or ensure ongoing learning within your organization?

Keep expectations high and realistic

Don't lower your expectations to meet your performance. Raise your level of performance to meet your expectations. Expect the best of yourself, and then do what is necessary to make it a reality. ~Ralph Marston

Whatever we expect with confidence becomes our own self-fulfilling prophecy. ~Brian Tracy

Expectations are what leaders use to guide current and future productivity within any organization. They must be reasonable, attainable, realistic, and connected to the work of the organization. Expectations are about citizenship, mutual respect, work ethic, and results. When guiding the work of the team, a leader must set the example for the standard of excellence in the workplace. Maintaining high expectations for yourself and the people you lead keeps the work focused on the vision and goals. Expectations need to be clear, fair, and realistic for people to experience success. Expectations need to match the reality of the job and sometimes need to be revisited and revised based on feedback, evaluation, and available resources.

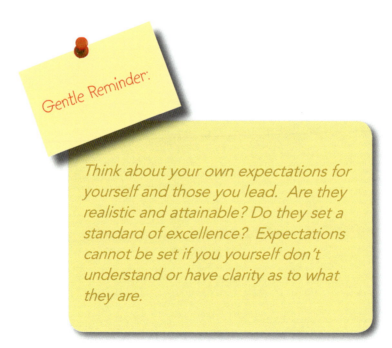

Gentle Reminder:

Think about your own expectations for yourself and those you lead. Are they realistic and attainable? Do they set a standard of excellence? Expectations cannot be set if you yourself don't understand or have clarity as to what they are.

Guide

Reflections:

- List five professional expectations for yourself.

- List five expectations of those you lead.

- What are the expectations of achieving results in your organization?

- Does the majority of your team rise to the expectations?

Sage on the stage vs. guide on the side

When the best leader's work is done the people say, 'We did it ourselves.'

~Lao Tzu

"Sage on the stage vs. guide on the side" is a saying I heard many years ago from a dear friend, colleague, and mentor Susan Kovalik. A "sage" is a profoundly wise person or an experienced person who has sound judgment. "Sage on the stage" is someone who shares their wisdom and experience by telling others about it. Front and center...alone, "on the stage", performing—imparting knowledge.

Having wisdom is a gift, being able to teach, model, and guide others is an even greater gift. The "guide on the side" is a wise or experienced person who works side by side with people...facilitating...coaching...and expecting people to use their own thinking, skills, and talents to make discoveries. The guide on the side encourages and supports people to be innovative in their craft. A leader who models strategies and expectations and limits the amount of just "talking about" strategies and expectations is truly a guide. There are times when the "sage on the stage" is needed but those times should never outweigh the time spent guiding on the side. When people are empowered to think for themselves, they feel valued, appreciated, and motivated to do their personal best.

Gentle Reminder:

Wisdom is applied knowledge.

Reflections:
- What skills must a leader have to be a guide on the side?

- Which do you do more . . . guide on the side or sage on the stage? Why?

- When is sage on the stage necessary in leadership?

Emotion vs. passion and professionalism

When dealing with people, remember you are not dealing with creatures of logic, but creatures of emotion. ~Dale Carnegie

When work, commitment, and pleasure all become one and you reach that deep well where passion lives, nothing is impossible. ~Unknown

There are, no doubt, people working with you who got into the line of work because of a "passion", talent, or an internal desire to do the work. Empowering leaders will foster and grow that passion and talent and encourage its development through ever-increasing challenges and opportunities, coupled with opportunities for lifelong learning. It is the job of leaders to take advantage of the enthusiasm, skill sets, knowledge, and experience that drive the work of their people.

Be aware of your passion and make sure you don't mix it with emotion. When guiding, remember to base responses on facts…do not let emotions drive your responses. If you find yourself taking things personally then take some time to step back, reflect on why you are reacting that way—separate your emotions from your core beliefs and values (it helps to write these down) and identify the facts of the situation before you respond. Guiding with heart is about maintaining professionalism at all times. No matter how you feel in any given situation your job is to maintain an air of professionalism—keep emotion (which includes inappropriate body talk) out of the mix.

"Never confuse emotion with passion" is a quote I wrote based on an experience I had during my principalship. What I found is that there are people who may not believe in the power of leading with heart…they may view it as being "emotional". They enjoy the benefits of working in an environment where people are valued (heart leadership) yet when something doesn't go their way they are the first to challenge. These are often people who do not have as much vested interest in a project or organization as you do. They will often confuse your heart energy, reactions, and proactive responses as emotion when in reality, it is the passion, the unwavering and unconditional love for the work, that drives the above traits. True passion cannot be diminished unless you allow it.

Gentle Reminder:

When emotions drive your responses, real issues become clouded and what really matters takes a back seat. Lead with passion and professionalism.

Reflections:

- Can you think of a time when you reacted emotionally instead of professionally?

- What was the circumstance?

- List your professional passions—which ones are most important?

- If someone were to ask you what your professional passions are, what would your response be?

- What does professional behavior entail?

Listen with a full heart, watch, and take notes

Your heart is your most important organ in the listening process. ~K. Cloke

It is the province of knowledge to speak, and it is the privilege of wisdom to listen. ~Oliver Wendell Holmes

If the person you are talking to doesn't appear to be listening, be patient. It may simply be that he has a small piece of fluff in his ear. ~Winnie the Pooh

Listening, not imitation, may be the sincerest form of flattery.
~Dr. Joyce Brothers

Give me the gift of a listening heart. ~King Solomon

Too many leaders think they are wonderful with people because they talk well. They don't realize that being wonderful with people means 'listening' well. ~Peter Drucker

An empowering leader should not be someone who comes in with their own agenda but someone who is willing to listen to what is needed and follow through based on the information gathered. Listening from the heart means that you give the person your undivided attention in the moment. It is a skill that many struggle with. It's a challenge to model good listening skills when you have so many other things on your plate. True listening can only happen if you concentrate on the conversation you are engaged with at the time. Full plates, pressing matters, and outside distractions can interfere with genuine listening. Everyone has a story to tell and it's challenging to listen when you also have something that needs to be said (or done).

To guide effectively, a leader with heart needs to know each team member—their experience, their approach to the work, what makes them tick. Leaders with heart learn about their team members and colleagues by listening, watching, and taking notes. Engaged listening is active listening and a skill most people need to improve upon. Often, people are so worried about what they want to say that they tend to only listen with one ear (half a heart). Thinking about what you want to say while another person is talking limits your ability to be objective or able to detect underlying themes, hidden agendas, or ulterior motives. In order to respond appropriately to an immediate situation, give the person your full heart, your full attention. Listen with your whole body and mind—that includes eye contact and appropriate body talk. Most people tend to be so ready to share or speak that they interrupt another person's story. Work hard at not interrupting—if you do interrupt—catch yourself, apologize, and let the person continue if appropriate.

Of course, interrupting and ending a conversation may sometimes be necessary due to someone who likes to hear themselves talk, or when there is disrespectful, threatening, or inappropriate behavior on the part of the person you are speaking with. If it's confrontational, count to ten before you respond. The discussion may be fact driven or may be driven by emotion – whatever the case give your full attention to the matter to prevent it from getting bigger. Keep the discussion in the lap of the one who has brought it to you. Listening with a full heart may entail asking for clarification so there are no misunderstandings. You may find you can contain the issue the moment it is shared if you give it your undivided attention. Listen with heart, stay true to your core beliefs and standards, and give a response that relates to the moment.

When you listen with heart you "wait your turn". Model conversational etiquette by making it a habit not to interrupt the person you are talking with, even if it is confrontational, and expect the same. Consider the source and facilitate the conversation without giving your opinion until the person has had their say. Take notes to help recall what has been shared and to demonstrate that the conversation is important to you.

He listens well who takes notes. ~Dante Alighieri

Taking notes while someone is talking is another way for the person to see that you are truly listening, engaged, and genuinely interested in what they have to say. When it's time for you to respond—use your notes as a guide. Use their words to rephrase statements made to ensure there are no misunderstandings.

Deep listening is miraculous for both listener and speaker. When someone receives us with open-hearted, non-judging, intensely interested listening, our spirits expand. ~Sue Patton Thoele

With listening comes watching...watch carefully the body talk of the person who is talking with you...focus and interpret what is really being said. Using a watchful eye along with active listening will provide a complete picture of the message being shared.

Gentle Reminders:

Active listening promotes a sense of caring and genuine interest in the topic being shared. When people feel they are being listened to they feel valued, which leads to personal best.

Real listening is something we all need to practice ...it is a gift that needs to be present during all conversations to ensure people feel respected and valued.

Reflections:

- What are the traits of a good listener?

- Do you consider yourself to be a good listener? Always?

- How do you handle distractions when they interfere with your ability to listen with a full heart?

- How do you eliminate bias when you listen?

- When you respond, do you reflect back and summarize what you have heard?

- What is your opinion about the impact eye contact and body language have during a conversation?

- What strategies do you use, in the moment, to help you remember what is being said?

- What are some strategies you could use to become a better listener?

Feedback – firm, inquisitive, thought-provoking

Feedback is an essential element to stay connected and responsive to your people. ~Laurie Hinzman

Feedback is the breakfast of champions. ~Ken Blanchard

An effective leader offers firm, inquisitive, and thought-provoking feedback where reflection, rather than reaction, is practiced, and self-evaluation is encouraged as a guiding light. Feedback engages people in conversations and serves as an avenue for sharing thoughts, questions, and concerns. The empowering leader must have the skill and expertise to observe, analyze, and give constructive feedback to enhance the organization's overall performance. Giving constructive feedback is a way to stay connected and responsive to the accomplishments and challenges of the people. Feedback should be immediate, focused on the issue at hand, and firm when needed. It is an accountability tool used to monitor and provide input into job performance. Feedback guides and keeps the work focused and on track. Without feedback, people would not know if they are reaching expected outcomes and goals.

When providing feedback, part of the process should include an element of self-evaluation by your team members. Self evaluation is a powerful way to encourage and expect people to reflect on their own abilities, actions, and skills. Self-evaluation needs to be honest and open about strengths, weaknesses, successes, and challenges. Providing people the opportunity to look into their own practice, letting them reflect, and be prepared to talk about it offers a chance for people to take responsibility for their own accomplishments and challenges. Carve out time for self-evaluation to be shared during your feedback debriefings.

On occasion, people will cast blame on others for situations they have created themselves. When giving feedback, make it a practice not to take on problems a team member has created. There will be times when a member who has created a problem, issue, or concern will try to turn the tables to make the issue become yours. They will blame everyone but themselves and make excuses as to why things went amiss. It is your job to discover the heart of the problem, keep the issues in their court, and guide them toward understanding that it was due to their decisions, their actions that led to the problem. People need to take responsibility for their own actions and need to be coached and held accountable for fixing their own mistakes.

Be direct and ask guiding questions that will encourage the person to recall the events that led up to the situation. Frame questions to always include their actions and help them see the difference between their current thinking and their actions. Connect actions to reactions as they relate to the problem. If defensiveness sets in, redirect that energy into having them justify why they are so defensive. (See the Voice chapter for more on defensiveness.) Stay calm and focused on the reality of who created the situation. Be supportive and guide them to finding solutions to the situation they have created.

Redirect with suggestions, accountability, and timelines

Accountability breeds response-ability. ~Stephen R. Covey

It is not only what we do, but also what we do not do, for which we are accountable. ~Molière

Even when a person does not acknowledge their mistakes, it needs to be made clear that some changes and corrective behavior are in order. Part of guiding includes providing support and remediation for those in need. If you have someone who is not doing their job, extenuating circumstances may be impacting their ability to perform at the level expected. Your job is to discover the heart of the problem. Gather the facts, gather the evidence, and set up support plans, action plans, or remediation plans to see if this person has the potential and wherewithal to do their job. If there isn't hope, then the guiding piece becomes firm and direct. This work doesn't have to be without heart.

Working with the facts will enable you to offer suggestions for next steps. Devise a plan collaboratively that will outline the specifics of the actions needed for improvement. Be clear and specific as to the actions and behaviors needed for change to occur. Steps need to be specific, few in number, and realistic. Do not overwhelm the remediation process by writing numerous steps for improvement—there should be a maximum of five steps outlined in the first phase of the support plan.

Accountability is key to ensuring change is truly occurring. Once specific next steps are outlined and agreed upon, a monitoring plan needs to be created.

Using the guiding process, set up a system that will keep you informed of changes being implemented. This system (which should include observations with immediate feedback) should be used to check progress towards achieving the goals set in the plan. Timelines for improvement need to be created that are reasonable and attainable if the person gives their full heart to the process.

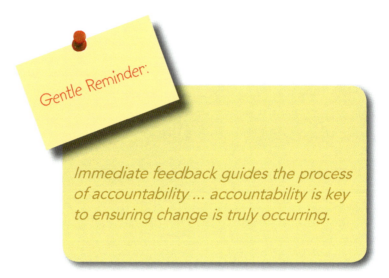

Gentle Reminder:

Immediate feedback guides the process of accountability ... accountability is key to ensuring change is truly occurring.

Reflections:

- What does immediate feedback mean to you?

- What's a reasonable timeframe for providing feedback?

- How do you provide feedback to your team members?

- How do you encourage the team to reflect on their own practices?

- How do you encourage people to do a self-evaluation before they meet with you for an evaluation or feedback debrief?

- What was the most difficult feedback you have ever had to give? What was the situation? What was the outcome?

- Have you had to write a remediation or support plan for a team member? Did the plan work —why or why not?

- How do you hold people responsible for their own actions?

- What are some strategies you use to remind people of their responsibilities for greatness?

Reflection

Step back, breathe, and take a moment to reflect on your choices, actions, and reactions of the day because tomorrow is a new day. ~Laurie Hinzman

A perfect reflection of the mind; this is the main way that you can perfect yourself. It is your duty and responsibility to learn from others. Take what is good from others, and incorporate it within yourself. Take what needs enhancing in others and enhance it within. ~Swami Sai Premananda

Reflection, one of my four "R's", is a life skill that can offer a new perspective on decisions made and actions taken. It is a powerful tool for analyzing and distinguishing between successes and failures, "might have beens", and "should have beens". Reflection lets you revisit and revise the outcomes of the day if necessary. It is also a time to acknowledge and validate your actions and behavior for the day. Reflection allows you to carefully consider or reconsider actions, options, and plans for next steps.

Reflection is a natural instinct because it is thoughtful remembering, and remembering is thinking. It's what we do with our reflections that make the difference. Reflection may take place throughout the day but is often more enlightening and clear when we are away from the workplace in a calm and quiet setting. It's important and beneficial to reflect with an open heart and a willingness to admit when change is in order.

True and effective reflection enables us to build upon successes, correct mistakes, and plan for challenges facing the organization. The ability to build upon the previous day will enable the organization to stay progressive and productive. Reflections are powerful because they are your thoughts, your thinking, your reasoning, your recollection, your pondering, your wondering, and your critiquing without any interference or interruptions from others. Personal reflections shape thoughts and empower you as the leader to come to work with a renewed or new perspective.

Gentle Reminder:

Taking time out of your busy life to reflect on your day provides clarity and a deeper understanding of the events of the day. The act of reflecting can either be written or organized in your mind—either way; it is an empowering tool for innovation, motivation, and change.

Reflections:

- How do you use reflection in your daily life?

- Do you take time away from work to reflect on your day?

- When do you find yourself reflecting the most?

- Where do you do your best thinking? How often do you get to that place?

- How do you organize your thinking—lists, computer, inside your head, etc.?

- In a perfect world, what would be the ideal place you could go to every day to reflect?

- Do you encourage others to use reflection when they are evaluating their work? How?

Reflection vs. reaction

Follow effective action with quiet reflection. From the quiet reflection will come even more effective action. ~James Levin

Action and reaction are equal and opposite. ~Gertrude Stein

An effective guiding practice is to reflect before you react to reoccurring situations that might be challenging. Reflecting (thinking) on the realities of the situation is what fuels the ability to arrive at a viable solution in a timely manner. An immediate reaction to a situation without verifying facts can be detrimental to the outcome. Take time for reflection by removing any emotion that might cloud judgment, and focus on fact gathering. Compartmentalize any stress and concerns of the situation by identifying emotions and facts. Create a t-chart that lists the positives and negatives to the situation. Document what has worked, is working, and what went wrong. With reflection it is also important to identify what is in your control and what isn't. Using written and/or mental reflection helps to organize your own thinking in preparation for your response. Being able to respond, using reflection as your guide, will enable you to remain focused on the real issues which will lead to faster and more effective solutions.

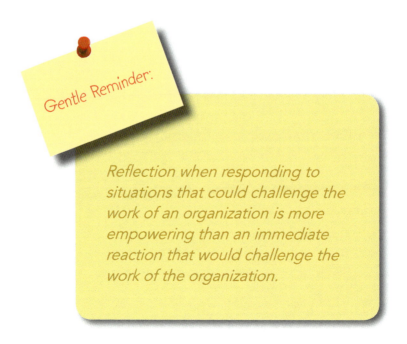

Gentle Reminder:

Reflection when responding to situations that could challenge the work of an organization is more empowering than an immediate reaction that would challenge the work of the organization.

Reflections:

- Can you think of a time when you reacted to a situation inappropriately because you didn't have all the facts? What was the outcome? If you could change how you reacted what steps would you implement?

- How do you define fact-finding?

- What are some strategies you could implement to prepare for response to a challenging situation?

confidence

Confidence, simply stated, is your heartfelt belief in YOU. ~*Laurie Hinzman*

We are all worms. But I believe that I am a glow-worm. ~ *Winston Churchill*

Success comes in cans, not can'ts. ~ *Unknown*

Confidence is believing in yourself, your skills, talents, and strengths. Confidence draws upon past and present experiences that shape your future experiences. It is tied to emotions and nurtured from an internal belief of certainty and self-worth. It is about having a firm belief in your own knowledge and abilities without displaying a sense of superiority or self-importance.

Confidence is exemplified through your approach and outlook when dealing with situations that draw upon your expertise. It is the ability to take action and make decisions that are most effective and in the best interests of the organization. Real confidence is self-assurance, which is the quality of trusting and having confidence in yourself and the decisions you make.

Part of the process of building self-confidence includes getting hit with an occasional rainstorm. You will encounter problems that will challenge your confidence level. There will be times when you lose faith and confidence in the system. The incompetence or lack of progressive practice from those you lead or those who lead you will get you down, try to make you feel inferior, or cast a shadow of doubt to your purpose and core beliefs. Keeping the heart in your confidence includes being able to dance in the rain. Confidence is emotional—emotion is part of the core of confidence.

When a storm hits and you start to question your ability, take time to reconnect with your inner self. Re-evaluate, reflect, and reaffirm your values and beliefs, experiences, and successes. Keep your confidence heart-healthy by confronting each storm with honesty and integrity—learning every step of the way. It's a genuinely confident person who comes through adversity with calm, dignity, and professionalism.

Confidence from the heart empowers leadership because it creates a work environment based on trustworthiness and belief in others' abilities. The leader who uses confidence with heart sets an example that gives permission for others to have confidence in themselves. To foster an environment where you and your team feel confident to do the work, consider the following areas:

- Experience
- Confidence without arrogance
- Nurture confidence in others
- Believe
- Lifelong learning
- Teachable moments

Experience

Your experiences can either nurture or challenge your self-confidence, the decision is yours. ~Laurie Hinzman

Experience is the knowledge and wisdom gained from your prior encounters, interactions, learning, and mistakes. It comes from events and practices that developed the skills and abilities you have today. Experience is the pipeline that fuels the confidence you have to be successful and accomplished in life and at your job. Experience drives your own self-confidence and also drives the success of any organization. It is essential you use your experience as a foundation for new learning that supports your growth and that of the organization. Experience is something that cannot be taken away but only built upon if you choose. Experiences, good or bad, can feed your confidence or tear it down—it is up to you to decide the outcome.

It's your responsibility to know the most effective and non-threatening way to share your expertise. There are times when experience is overlooked or under-appreciated by those at the top. Don't let that stop you from using what you know to stay focused and on target for achieving the vision and goals of the organization. Experience can serve as a model for excellence when it is presented without self-righteousness. Experience that promotes success within your organization isn't just about you, it's about the collective knowledge within your organization. Be confident because of your experience, not in spite of. Use your expertise and the experience of others to build an organization of achievements and results.

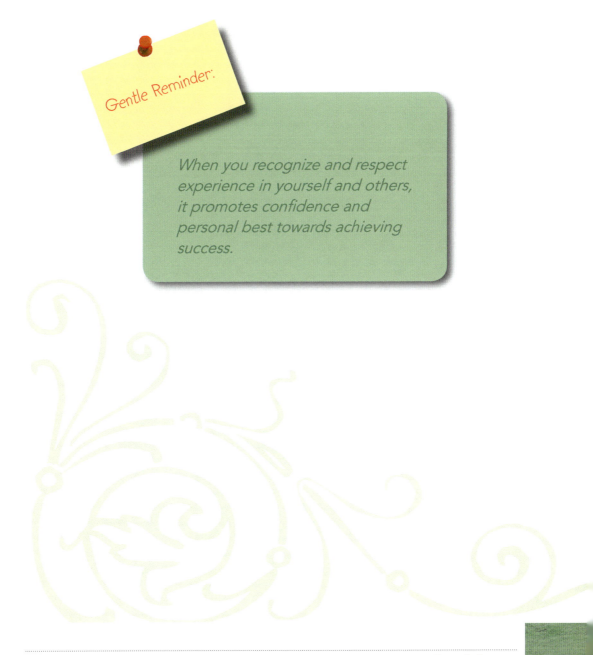

Gentle Reminder:

When you recognize and respect experience in yourself and others, it promotes confidence and personal best towards achieving success.

Reflections:

- When did you last update your resume?

- Have you ever created a list of all your experiences?

- Take time to create a list that reflects your lifelong experiences that have led to where you are today.

- How does your current job nurture your experiences?

- Do you feel appreciated and acknowledged for your experience? Why or why not?

- What are the experience levels of your team members—collectively and individually?

- Create an inventory of experiences within the organization.

- Are you using (taking advantage of) the experiences your team members and superiors have to offer?

- Create a chart that categorizes the levels of expertise of your team (include areas of expertise, number of years, and are they in a job that promotes their expertise).

Confidence without arrogance

A successful person can catch stones thrown at them and use them to build a bridge. ~Laurie Hinzman

A truly confident leader will lead with heart, not ego. ~Laurie Hinzman

Confidence is about how comfortable you are on the inside and out. An effective leader will build and possess confidence without a display of arrogance. Confidence is not the same as arrogance. In fact, arrogance gets in the way of your ability to use your best judgment whereas confidence feeds your ability. Confidence and arrogance tend to negate one another.

Confidence is a great thing and should be treated as such. It's what you do with your confidence that matters. There is a difference between believing in and trusting your own abilities and the act of "convincing" others that they should believe in you—it's how you differentiate between the two that is up to you. It's important to keep your confidence heart-healthy, which means to keep boastfulness and self-righteousness out of the picture.

Arrogance is a negative force that will impact, if not impede, effectiveness and efficiency in the workplace. In an environment where integrity is an expectation among all team members, there is no room for arrogance. When people chat about how great they are (air of superiority or greater than thou attitude), ask yourself—who are they trying to convince—themselves or me? When people feel the need to tell others what they know, how much money they make, or how great they are, they are either on the defensive (see the Voice chapter) or they are trying to convince their friends and colleagues. It demonstrates an elitist and superior attitude. Arrogant people are often covering for their own low self-esteem. If these people were truly confident and comfortable in their own skin, then they wouldn't have to waste their energies on convincing others.

Gentle Reminder:

Arrogance is presumptuous boastfulness . . . your non-arrogant actions and follow-through are the telltale indicator of your skills, experience, wisdom, and knowledge—go confidently with conviction and certitude.

Confidence

Reflections:
- What does confidence mean to you?

- Describe your understanding of your own confidence.

- Think about how often you talk about yourself…what are the circumstances when you do?

- What is the difference between confidence and being an expert in your field?

- How do emotions impact your confidence and that of others?

- How do you respond to people when they have paid you a compliment?

- How do you respond when someone pays the organization a compliment?

- Re-evaluate your core beliefs and values—make a list to serve as a gentle reminder when the rain comes.

- Have you had your expertise challenged recently? Who challenged it? How did you handle it?

- Make a list of the people who are boastful and talk highly of themselves—do they work with you?

Nurture confidence in others

If you believe in the words "I can't" then it's you who will put their meaning into play. ~Laurie Hinzman

A good leader inspires others with confidence in him; a great leader inspires others with confidence in themselves. ~Unknown

One of the most empowering things a leader can do is build the self-confidence in those they lead. To successfully build and nurture the confidence of others, you must first have a full understanding of your own confidence. Using your own self-confidence to model, teach, facilitate, and promote self-worth within the organization will result in people wanting to work harder and give their personal best. Building self-confidence in others is an unselfish gift from the heart. Building confidence in others also boosts morale which enriches any environment. Making it a consistent practice will create a work atmosphere where people feel valued, appreciated, and want to come to work.

The act of building confidence in others is about positive and supportive interactions. Everyone loves to be honored, applauded, or thanked for the work they have done. Fostering a positive, "you can" attitude among your team is heart-healthy leadership. When people feel good about what they do, nothing can stop them from being innovative and productive. In an effort to foster growth, avoid trying to fit everyone into the same mold. Recognize individuality and encourage creative flight in those you trust. Be positive in your approach to all situations. Address negativity with energy and a quest to return it positively. When negative comments are made, they are often a reflection of a belief system. When one believes they can't or that others can't, then in "those eyes", in that moment, they won't. Helping others to see the good things they have to offer will contribute greatly to the overall success of the organization. When people feel you believe in them and their capabilities, they will believe in themselves, trust you as their leader, and produce results with passion and dedication. When people believe in themselves, individually and collectively, results happen.

Your own confidence and positive attitude will be an inspiration to others. As we allow our own light to shine, respectfully, we unconsciously give permission for others to do the same (adapted from *A Return to Love* by Marianne Williamson).

Gentle Reminder:

Confidence in ourselves grows as we receive compliments for the work we have done.

Confidence

Reflections:

- Do you believe it's important to build the self-confidence of your team? Why or why not?

- How do you build confidence in the people you lead?

- Identify and list the knowledgeable people in your organization who need self-esteem support.

Believe

Believe in yourself. You gain strength, courage, and confidence by every experience in which you stop to look fear in the face. You must do that which you think you cannot do. ~Eleanor Roosevelt

You'll see it when you believe it. ~Wayne Dyer

Share the power . . . plans don't accomplish the work, people do. You have to believe your people are competent and that every job is important.

~Colin Powell

Believing is essential to confidence. Your own beliefs facilitate and drive the work. You must believe in yourself, your team, and in the value of the work you are doing now and where it will lead—personally and professionally. When you truly believe in the people you work with they will believe in you as their leader. Believing in your mission, its relevance and its probability for achievement, is a key element in success. Mutual belief between a leader and the team is the foundation for collegiality and collaboration grounded in shared core values and understandings. Believing in your own ability to successfully produce results creates the basis for personal best accomplishments which reflect high moral and ethical standards.

A leader who believes in their own expertise and that of others will facilitate the implementation of strategies that are progressive and address the goals and objectives developed by the group's collaborative efforts. Stay current, stay progressive, and believe you can lead with heart.

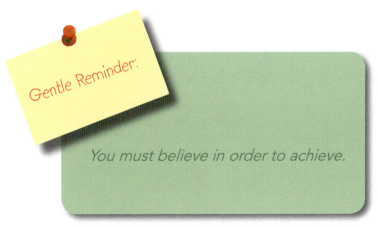

Gentle Reminder:

You must believe in order to achieve.

Reflections:

- What core beliefs drive your work?

- In what ways are your beliefs aligned with your integrity?

- What is the difference between belief and trust?

- Are your beliefs and actions based on data or intuition (situational)? Which plays a larger role in your decision-making process and why?

- In what ways do you believe the people you lead have the ability to produce results?

- Describe excellence and personal best. What do you expect of yourself and others on a daily basis? Do you come to work with a full heart expecting excellence and personal best from yourself and others?

Lifelong learning

Every moment counts because every moment is a teachable moment.
~Laurie Hinzman

Commit yourself to lifelong learning. The most valuable asset you'll ever have is your mind and what you put into it. ~Brian Tracy

Lifelong learning enhances any work environment. You gain strength, courage, and confidence whenever you choose to learn from an experience. Confidence isn't about knowing everything, it's about realizing that you don't know everything. It's about being open to new ideas, suggestions, and your own professional growth. For your confidence level to stay strong, there must be continuous growth through continuous learning and discovery. Learning needs to be a lifelong commitment for personal growth, especially while you are responsible for the health and welfare of the organization you lead. Learning enriches the impact that experiences have on your self-esteem and life. Without a commitment to lifelong learning, people become stagnant—complacent. Status quo permeates the environment because people, including you, become comfortable.

Lifelong learning is a confidence builder. It's about taking what you know, applying it to what you have just learned, and using it for next steps with confidence and heart. Not only does learning build upon what you know, it gives you confidence to share that knowledge with others in support of their own learning. Continuous learning keeps you on the cutting edge, making you credible and marketable. New learning is a support system for maintaining and growing confidence. You are in charge of expanding your own knowledge base. When new learning has stopped for you, as the leader, then new learning has stopped for all team members. Make it your responsibility to seek new knowledge, through experts and research, even if it takes you outside the organization.

Gentle Reminder:

New knowledge can either challenge our comfort zones, leaving our confidence vulnerable; or validate and build upon the work we are currently doing, feeding our confidence. Keeping confidence well-educated and informed will open doors to promising possibilities.

Reflections:

- When was the last time you attended a meeting where you experienced new learning?

- How did the new learning help you facilitate greatness within your organization?

- What professional publications do you read? How often?

- What research do you use to guide your leadership practice?

- Do you know everything? If not, what do you hope to learn next as it relates to your job? As it relates to life?

Confidence

Teachable moments

One has to have the skill and foresight to alter plans to capture moments that will expose, engage, and expand the knowledge of others. ~Laurie Hinzman

Insanity is doing the same thing over and over again but expecting different results. ~Rita Mae Brown

When you remember that entire lives are built from individual moments, you can understand the importance and value of a "teachable moment". Teachable moments are situations or events that happen without being planned... they just happen. Teachable moments are "in the moment" occasions for learning, creativity, discovery, and innovation. They are random, unexpected, and have a short window of opportunity. These experiences are usually unrelated to the immediate task but could give new knowledge and insight into another or future task. Teachable moments are reactions to a situation you haven't planned and instead of ignoring it, you incorporate it. To ignore them is to close the door on an opportunity for expanded or new learning.

As a leader with heart, it is not just an option, but an imperative, to engage in "teachable moments". New or expanded "in the moment" learning can offer a chance to model and see things in a different way. However, to capitalize on teachable moments, you must be flexible. Leaders who are experts in their field can turn any spur of the moment event into a lesson. With our busy schedules and the flight of time, many opportunities for learning have a tendency to pass us by. It is the flexible leader who makes the time to take advantage of those moments.

Gentle Reminder:

Teachable moments are experiences that should not escape our attention. They are moments when our awareness or understanding of something becomes stronger. They are moments that inadvertently capture our attention and offer a chance for us to experience new learning.

Reflections:

- Think about when you have been in a meeting with your team or in the middle of a presentation and you had to alter your agenda and plans to address a teachable moment. What was that moment and how did you address it?

- Think of and list some examples of teachable moments that your team has experienced. What new learning came from the moments?

Made in the USA
Charleston, SC
06 February 2013